Zaha Hadid: Nabern

Zaha Hadid: Nabern

Arthotel Billie Strauß, Kirchheim-Nabern

Einführung/Introduction
Paul Sigel

Edition Axel Menges

ISBN 3-930698-64-1

Englische Übersetzung/English translation:
Michael Robinson

Gestaltung/Design: Axel Menges

Printed in Korea.

Inhalt

Contents

Floating buildings. Almost

»When I did the Hong Kong Peak, I almost believed there was such a thing as zero gravity. I can now believe that buildings can float. I know they don't, but I almost believe it.« Zaha Hadid

Zwischen zwei denkmalgeschützten Fachwerkbauten inmitten des pittoresken schwäbischen Dorfes Nabern soll nach einem Entwurf Zaha Hadids eine ungewöhnliche skulpturale Form, die sich kontrastreich gegen die Umgebung absetzen und alltägliche Architekturerfahrungen provokant in Frage stellen will, in das Blickfeld des Betrachters rücken. Zaha Hadids Modell des geplanten Erweiterungsbaus für das Arthotel Billie Strauß von 1992 zeigt verzerrte geometrische Formen wie Ellipse, Kreuz, Spirale und Stern, die in vertikaler Anordnung eine turmartige Skulptur bilden, gerahmt von einem filigranen Stahlgerüst. Die kreuzartige und die sternförmige Großform sollen als in sich abgeschlossene Zimmer des Hotels dienen, die durch eine spiralartige Treppe untereinander verbunden werden. Die teilweise in ein Wasserbecken versenkte ellipsoide Basis der Skulptur, der bereits realisierte »Blobby«, wird unter anderem für Veranstaltungen des Arthotels genutzt. Ein auf der Höhe der Treppenspirale angesetzter Steg bindet das Projekt an den links gelegenen Altbau an, der den ersten Bauabschnitt des Hotels bildet.

Bereits seit Anfang der 80er Jahre betreiben die Galeristin Billie Strauß und ihr Mann, der Architekt Manfred Strauß, in dem Fachwerkbau des ehemaligen Dorfrathauses ein Restaurant, zu dem sich seit Anfang 1994 das Arthotel in dem links daneben liegenden Altbau gesellte. Bei vollständigem Erhalt der Fachwerksubstanz präsentiert sich der Innenausbau des Hotels, der in Zusammenarbeit von Zaha Hadid mit dem Ehepaar Strauß entworfen und umgesetzt wurde, als expressiver Gegenentwurf zu der historischen Schale des Gebäudes. Verzerrtgesprengte Grundrisse, raumdurchstoßende Flächen und farbenfrohes Design stehen in extravagantem Kontrast zur Idyllik des Fachwerkbaus und stellen die experimentierfreudige Kreativität des kooperierenden Trios unter Beweis. Das Erweiterungsprojekt von 1992 soll diese Spannung der Widersprüche nun in ein architektonisches Ensemble von Alt-, Neu-, Altbau ausdehnen.

Fast unsichtbar durchbohren mikadodünne Stützen die architektonische Skulptur und bilden einen letzten Verankerungspunkt für die nahezu schwebende A-Logik der ansonsten scheinbar der Schwerkraft entzogenen einzelnen Baukörper. Klassische Ordnungsstrukturen wie tektonischer Aufbau, oben und unten, vorne und hinten versagen angesichts dieser Architektur. Statt dessen provoziert die Inszenierung vieldimensionale Blickperspektiven, sie erfordert Annäherung und Durchgang, um den Raum zwischen den Formen, die vertikale und die horizontale Dimension zu erfassen. Angesichts der frech flottierenden Körper erscheint die filigrane Orthogonalität des Rahmengerüsts als ironischer Kommentar zur Hinlänglichkeit physikalischer Zwänge und vitruvianischer Ordnungslogik.

Die einzelnen Elemente von Zaha Hadids Entwurf deuten auf grundlegende und zentrale Topoi ihrer architektonischen Motivik und ihres expressiven Gestus hin. Es ist eine Architektur, deren Elemente den Kräften der Gravitation zu entgehen scheinen, die einem konventionellen tektonischen Aufbau provokant widersprechend entgegentritt, deren zerdehnte und überlängte geometrische Grundformen, Keile und Balken, Räume eher durchschneiden denn begrenzen und dadurch Raum, Grenze, Spannung und Leere in einer neuen Weise sinnlich erlebbar machen. Deutlich setzt sich die Architektin mit dem Vorbild russischer Suprematisten und Konstruktivisten auseinander. Ihre Modelle und mehr noch ihre »Paintings« erscheinen als Wiederaufnahme und Fortführung von Themen, die die russische und frühe sowjetische Avantgarde Anfang des Jahrhunderts in Malerei und utopischen Architekturentwürfen formulierte. In der suprematistischen Malerei von Kasimir Malewitsch und den »Proun«-Bildern von El Lissitzky oder in den dreidimensionalen konstruktivistischen Objekten von Gustav Kluzis und Wladimir Tatlin feierte die Begeisterung für die revolutionären wissenschaftlich-technischen, aber auch sozialrevolutionären Potentiale der Moderne ein fulminantes Zukunftscredo. Jenseits tradierter physikalischer Logik und Systematik visionierten die Konstruktivisten eine neue Wirklichkeit, die außerhalb heutiger rationaler Vermeßbarkeit und mathematischer Logik angesiedelt sein sollte. In der suprematistischen Malerei von Malewitsch gibt es keine eindeutigen perspektivischen Bezüge mehr, seine scheinbar reinen und objektiven geometrischen Formen werden in räumlich unklare Beziehungen gesetzt. Die Logik der Form erscheint in alogischen irrationalen Raumbeziehungen, die Formen beginnen in einem nicht zu definierenden Raum zu schweben.

In der Auseinandersetzung mit und in Analogie zu Themen der russischen Avantgarde steht Zaha Hadid in einer Reihe mit einigen anderen Architekten, die darüber hinaus auch auf weiteren Ebenen Entsprechungen aufweisen. Architekten wie Peter Eisenman, Bernard Tschumi, Rem Koolhaas oder Daniel Libeskind zeigen auch Analogien, was ihren generellen Zugang zu Architektur, Raum und Ordnungshierarchien an-

1. Das Arthotel Billie Strauß von Westen.

1. The Arthotel Billie Strauß from the west.

Floating buildings. Almost

»When I did the Hong Kong Peak, I almost believed there was such a thing as zero gravity. I can now believe that buildings can float. I know they don't, but I almost believe it.« Zaha Hadid

Zaha Hadid has designed an unusual sculptural form to be built as an eyecatcher between two listed half-timbered buildings in the middle of the picturesque Swabian village of Nabern. It is intended to form a contrast with its surroundings and address provocative questions to everyday architectural experience. Zaha Hadid's model for the planned extension to Billie Strauß's 1992 Arthotel is made up of distorted geometrical shapes like ellipse, cross, spiral and star. They are arranged vertically to form a tower-like sculpture, framed by filigree steel scaffolding. The cross- and star-like structures are intended to serve as separate rooms in the hotel; they will be connected by a spiral staircase. The ellipsoid base of the sculpture, the »blobby« that has already been realized, partially sunk in a pool of water, will be used among other things for events at the hotel. A bridge set on the level of the spiral staircase links the project to the older building on the left, the first phase of the hotel.

Gallery-owner Billie Strauß and her husband, architect Manfred Strauß, have been running a wine bar in the half-timbered former village town hall since the early eighties. This was joined by the Arthotel in the old building on the left in early 1994. The half-timbered building has been retained in its entirety, and the interior arrangement of the hotel, designed and realized by Zaha Hadid with Billie and Manfred Strauß, is an expressive counter-design to the historical shell of the building. Distorted and exploded ground plans, surfaces that break through space and design that revels in colour present an extravagant contrast with the idyllic half-timbered building and prove the experimental gusto and creativity of the co-operating trio. The 1992 extension project is intended to bring this exciting set of contradictions into an architectural ensemble of old, new and old buildings.

Stays as thin as spills thrust through the architectural sculpture almost invisibly, forming a last anchorage for the almost floating a-logicality of the individual buildings, which otherwise apparently defy gravity. Classical ordering devices like tectonic structure, top and bottom, in front and behind break down when confronted with this architecture. Instead the arrangement provokes multi-dimensional perspectives, demands to be approached and walked through in order to grasp the space between the shapes, the vertical and the horizontal dimension. The filigree rectangularity of the framework seems like an ironic commentary on the adequacy of physical constraints and the logic of Vitruvian order when confronted with the insolently floating bodies.

The individual elements of Zaha Hadid's design point to fundamental and central topoi of her architectural motifs and her expressive gesture. This is architecture whose elements seem to defy the force of gravity, provocatively confronting conventional tectonic structure in order to contradict it. Its painfully extended, excessively long geometrical shapes, wedges and beams cut through rather than border rooms and thus lay space, border, tension and emptiness open to sensual experience in an entirely new way. The architect is clearly coming to terms with the model of the Russian Suprematists and Constructivists. Her models and even more her »Paintings« seem to return to and continue themes formulated by the Russian and early Soviet avant-garde in painting and utopian architecture in the early years of the century.
In Kasimir Malevich's Suprematist painting and El Lissitzsky's »Proun« pictures, or in three-dimensional Constructivist objects by Gustav Kluzis and Vladimir Tatlin, enthusiasm for the revolutionary scientific and technical but also social-revolutionary potential of Modernism celebrated a brilliant credo for the future. The Constructivists had a vision of a new reality beyond traditional logic and systems that lay outside prevailing measurability and mathematical logic. Malevich's Suprematist painting no longer has unambiguous perspective, its apparently pure and objective geometrical shapes are placed in relationships that are spatially unclear. The logic of the form appears in a-logical irrational spatial relationships and the forms begin to float in a space that cannot be defined.

In coming to terms with and by analogy with the themes of the Russian avant-garde, Zaha Hadid is part of a series of other architects who show correspondences beyond this on other planes. Architects like Peter Eisenman, Bernard Tschumi, Rem Koolhaas or Daniel Libeskind also show analogous behaviour as far as their general approach to architecture, space and the hierarchy of order are concerned. Despite a complete independence of gesture they are all linked by the fact that they reject architecture as an unambiguously valid expression of hierarchy and elemental order.

In 1988 these structural correspondences were identified and categorized as »Deconstructivist architecture« as part of an exhibition in the New York Museum of Modern Art, conceived by the father of Modernism, Philip Johnson, working with Marc Wigley. Despite all

belangt. Sie alle verbindet trotz eines vollkommen eigenständigen Gestus die Ablehnung von Architektur als eindeutig gültigem Ausdruck von Hierarchie und elementarer Ordnung.

Diese strukturellen Entsprechungen wurden 1988 im Rahmen einer Ausstellung im New Yorker Museum of Modern Art, die vom Altvater der Moderne, Philip Johnson, zusammen mit Marc Wigley konzipiert wurde, unter dem Label »Dekonstruktivistische Architektur« thematisiert und kategorisiert. Bei aller Problematik einer derartigen Etikettierung kann die Annäherung an den Begriff Dekonstruktivismus doch eine partielle Klärung der grundlegenden Fragen erbringen. Zum einen deutet »De-Konstruktivismus« auf einen der historischen Bezugspunkte dieser Architektur hin. Zum anderen verweist der Begriff auf sensible strukturelle Analogien zur dekonstruktiven Philosophie von Jacques Derrida.

Derridas Textkritik zeigt Dekonstruktion als Schichtarbeit, die das Konstrukt scheinbar rationaler Argumentationslogik reflektiert und klassische Begriffshierarchien offenlegt. Durch die Infragestellung erratischer, geradezu mythischer Wertebegriffe artikuliert er Aporien innerhalb hieratischer Prinzipien rationalen Denkens. Dabei formuliert Derrida keineswegs antiaufklärerische Manifeste; vielmehr steht seine Reflexion in einer langen Tradition vernunftskritischen Denkens, das immer auch notwendiges Korrektiv selbstherrlicher Ratio und funktionaler Ökonomie war. Dem in sich stimmig Homogenen wird das widersprüchlich Heterogene entgegengestellt.

Die Analogie zwischen philosophischer Reflexion und strukturierendem Bauen und Fügen rückt Derridas Argumentation in die Nähe architektonischen Denkens. Rationale »Begriffsgebäude« werden de-konstruiert, Derrida spricht in diesem Zusammenhang von »Ab-Auf-Bau«. Die Berechtigung oder gar die Existenz einer wahren und gültigen Ordnung von stabilen Gedankenstrukturen wird in Frage gestellt.

So können Peter Eisenmans »De-Komposition« klassischer moderner Architekturformen oder Bernard Tschumis Begriff der architektonischen »Disjunktion«, der Auföšung klassischer Kompositionsregeln, als strukturelle Entsprechungen zu philosophischen Überlegungen angesehen werden. Dem Schwebezustand einer destabilisierten Gedankenlogik kann eine antihierarchische und schwebende Architektur zugeordnet werden.

Zaha Hadids Architekturvisionen als Auseinandersetzung mit aufgelösten Strukturordnungen, als scheinbar chaotische Überlagerung von Formen und als Gegenthese zu physikalischen Notwendigkeiten der Gravitation stehen genau im Schnittpunkt der Berührung von philosophischerkenntnistheoretischer Spekulation und bildlicharchitektonischer Gestaltung. Das Paradoxon und der Bruch werden nicht nur zugelassen, sondern kraftvoll inszeniert und lustvoll genossen.

Im Gegensatz zu den konstruktivistischen Archetypen von Malewitsch, El Lissitzky und Tatlin formuliert Zaha Hadid kein revolutionäres Manifest einer neuen Weltordnung der Zukunft. Nach den Erfahrungen von Weltkriegen, Atombomben, ökologischen Katastrophen, Entfremdung und Isolation bietet das ausgehende 20. Jahrhundert keine Projektionsfläche mehr für einen ungebrochenen Glauben an beständige Optimierung und Humanisierung der Lebenswelten durch technisch-wissenschaftlichen Fortschritt. Wo Tatlin 1920 noch eine dynamische Spiral-Turm-Architektur als Denkmal für die Drit-Kommunistische Internationale entwarf, konterkariert Zaha Hadids Turmentwurf mit seiner spannungsvollen Instabilität jegliche Projektion von selbstgewissem Zukunftsoptimismus.

Die Zeiten, in denen Zaha Hadid und ihre Kollegen vorwiegend als spekulative Künstlerarchitekten abgelehnt wurden, sind vorbei. Nachdem sie jahrelang durch theoretische Äußerungen und Projektpräsentationen die architektonische Diskussion provokant mitgeprägt hatten, findet sich seit einigen Jahren eine zunehmende Bereitschaft seitens verschiedener Auftraggeber, sich auf das experimentelle Abenteuer einzulassen. Nachdem Bernard Tschumi seit Mitte der 80er Jahre an der Realisierung des Pariser Parc de la Villette arbeitete, Daniel Libeskind in Berlin das Jüdische Museum baut und Frank Gehry unter anderem das Vitra-Museum in Weil am Rhein realisieren konnte, rückte mittlerweile auch Zaha Hadid mit konkreten Projekten und realisierten Bauten in den Vordergrund. Seit ihrer prämierten Projektstudie für einen Jet-Set-Club auf dem Hong Kong Peak von 1982 fanden ihre Arbeiten zunehmend Akzeptanz. Obwohl sie immer wieder kurz vor Eintritt in die Realisationsphase verschiedene Projekte auf Grund der Skepsis der Auftraggeber aufgeben mußte, gelang es ihr mittlerweile, mit dem Moon Soon Restaurant in Sapporo und dem Vitra-Feuerwehrhaus in Weil am Rhein in der Nachbarschaft von Frank Gehry und Tadao Ando eindrucksvolle Belege für die Baubarkeit von Visionen zu präsentieren, ohne einen Verlust an Spannung in Kauf nehmen zu müssen. Es scheint, als ob die »Zeit der Unschuld« der Kunstwerke auf dem Papier, vorüber sei. Ein Projekt wie der Erweiterungsbau des Arthotels Billie Strauß, eine Verbindung von »folly« und alltäglicher Nutzbarkeit, stellt nun eine weitere reizvolle Herausforderung und Chance dar, Authentizität und Poesie einer schwebenden Architektur unter Beweis zu stellen.

2. Wladimir Tatlin, Denkmal der Dritten Internationale, Moskau, 1920, Projekt.

2. Vladimir Tatlin, Monument to the Third International, Moscow, 1920, project.

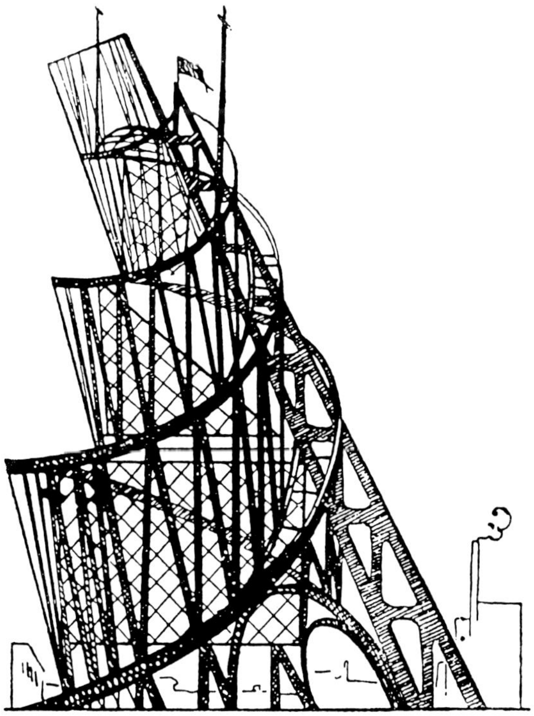

the problems raised by labelling of this kind an approach to the concept of Deconstructivism does produce a partial explanation of the fundamental questions. On the one hand, »De-Constructivism« points to one of these architects' historical reference points. On the other hand the concept indicates sensitive structural analogies with Jacques Derrida's Deconstructivist philosophy.

Derrida's textual criticism shows Deconstruction as layered work that reflects the construct of apparently rational logical argument and reveals classical conceptual hierarchies. By questioning erratic, almost mythical value concepts he articulates aporia within the hieratic principles of rational thought. But Derrida is by no means formulating anti-enlightenment manifestos: his reflections are in a long tradition of thought-criticizing reason that was always a necessary corrective to high-handed reason and functional economy. Something consistently homogeneous is confronted with contradictory heteronomy.

The analogy between philosophical reflection and structuring building and jointing shifts Derrida's argument close to architectural thinking. Rational »conceptual edifices« are deconstructed. In this context Derrida talks of »de-re-construction«. The justification and also the existence of a true and valid order of stable thought structures is called into question.

Thus Peter Eisenman's »de-composition« of classical Modern architectural forms or Bernard Tschumi's concept of architectural »disjunction«, the removal of classical rules of composition, can be seen as structural correspondences with philosophical considerations. Anti-hierarchical and floating architecture can be classified within the floating condition of destabilized thought-logic.

Zaha Hadid's architectural visions as an analysis of dissolved structural orders, as an apparently chaotic overlapping of forms and as a counter-thesis to the physical necessities of gravity, are precisely at the interface of contact between philosophical and epistemological speculation and pictorial and architectural creativity. The paradox and the break are not just admitted, but powerfully staged and enjoyed with relish.

In contrast with the Constructivist archetypes of Malevich, El Lissitzky and Tatlin, Zaha Hadid is not formulating a revolutionary manifesto of a new world order for the future. After the experience of world wars, atom bombs, ecological catastrophes, alienation and isolation the late 20th century no longer offers an area for projecting unbroken faith in constant optimization and humanization of life-worlds through technical and scientific progress. In 1920 Tatlin could still design dynamic spiral tower architecture as a memorial to the Third Communist International, but Zaha Hadid's tower design with its tension-filled instability undermines any projection of self-confident optimism about the future.

The times in which Zaha Hadid and her colleagues were largely rejected as speculative art-architects have passed. After helping to shape architectural argument provocatively for years with theoretical statements and project presentations, various clients have for some years now been showing increasing readiness to take part in the experimental adventure. After commissions like Bernard Tschumi's successful work on the Parc de la Villette in Paris from the mid 80s onwards, Daniel Libeskind's Jewish Museum in Berlin and Frank Gehry's Vitra Museum in Weil am Rhein, Zaha Hadid has moved into the foreground with concrete projects and realized buildings. Since her prize-winning project study for a jet-set club on Hong Kong Peak in 1982 her work met with increasing acceptance. Although she has repeatedly had to abandon projects shortly before the realization phase because of clients' scepticism, she has in the mean time, with the Mon Soon Restaurant in Sapporo and the Vitra fire-station in Weil am Rhein, near to Frank Gehry and Tadao Ando, successfully provided impressive proof that visions can be built without having to accept any loss of tension. It therefore seems as though the »age of innocence«, the works of art on paper, has passed. A project like the extension to Billie Strauß's Arthotel, a combination of »folly« and everyday usefulness, now presents another attractive challenge and an opportunity to prove the authenticity and poetry of floating architecture.

S. 10/11
1. »Painting« des Turmes, Frühjahr 1992.

p. 10/11
1. »Painting« of the tower, spring 1992.

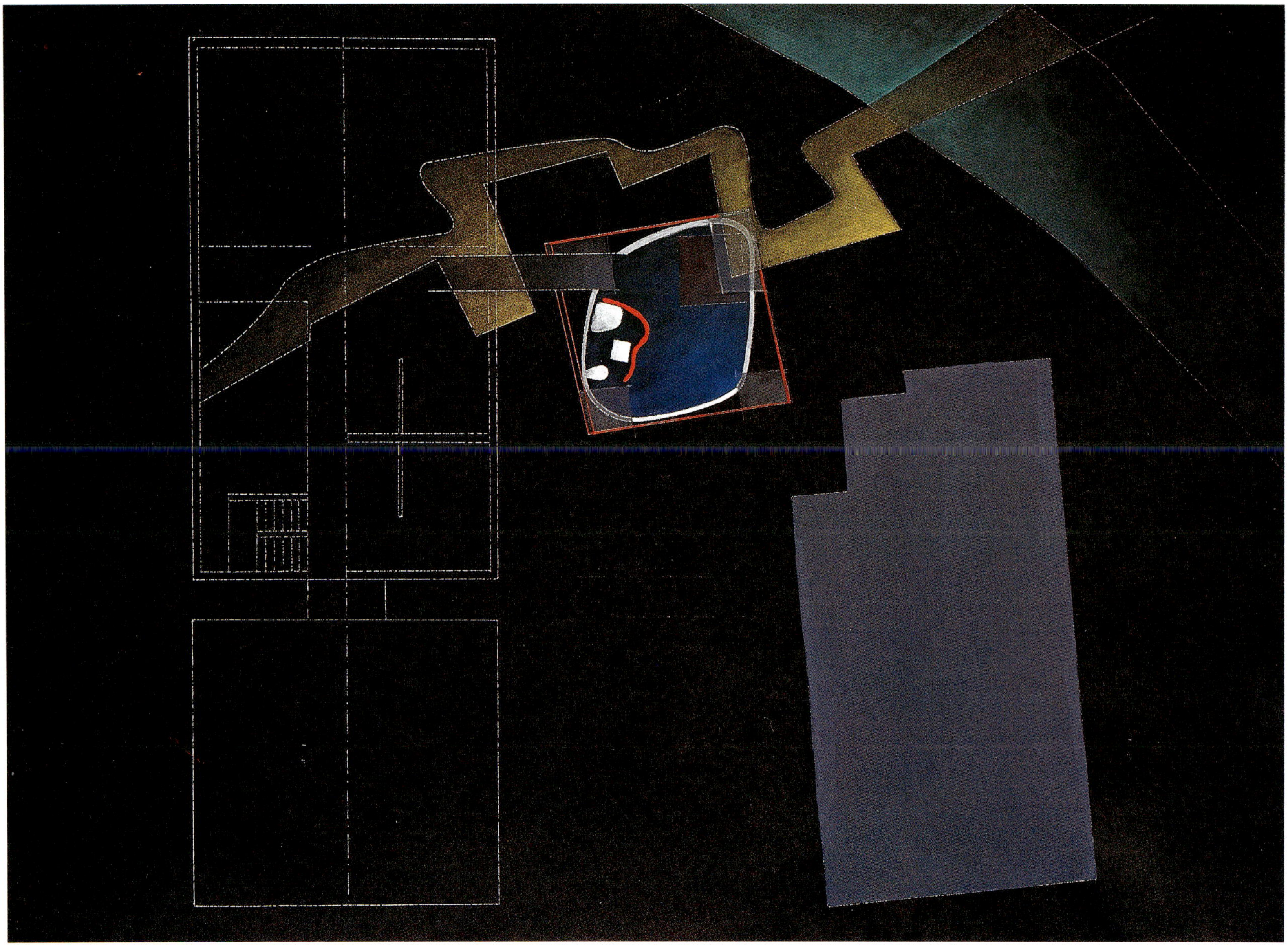

2, 3. »Paintings« des Turmes, Frühjahr 1992.

2, 3. »Paintings« of the tower, spring 1992.

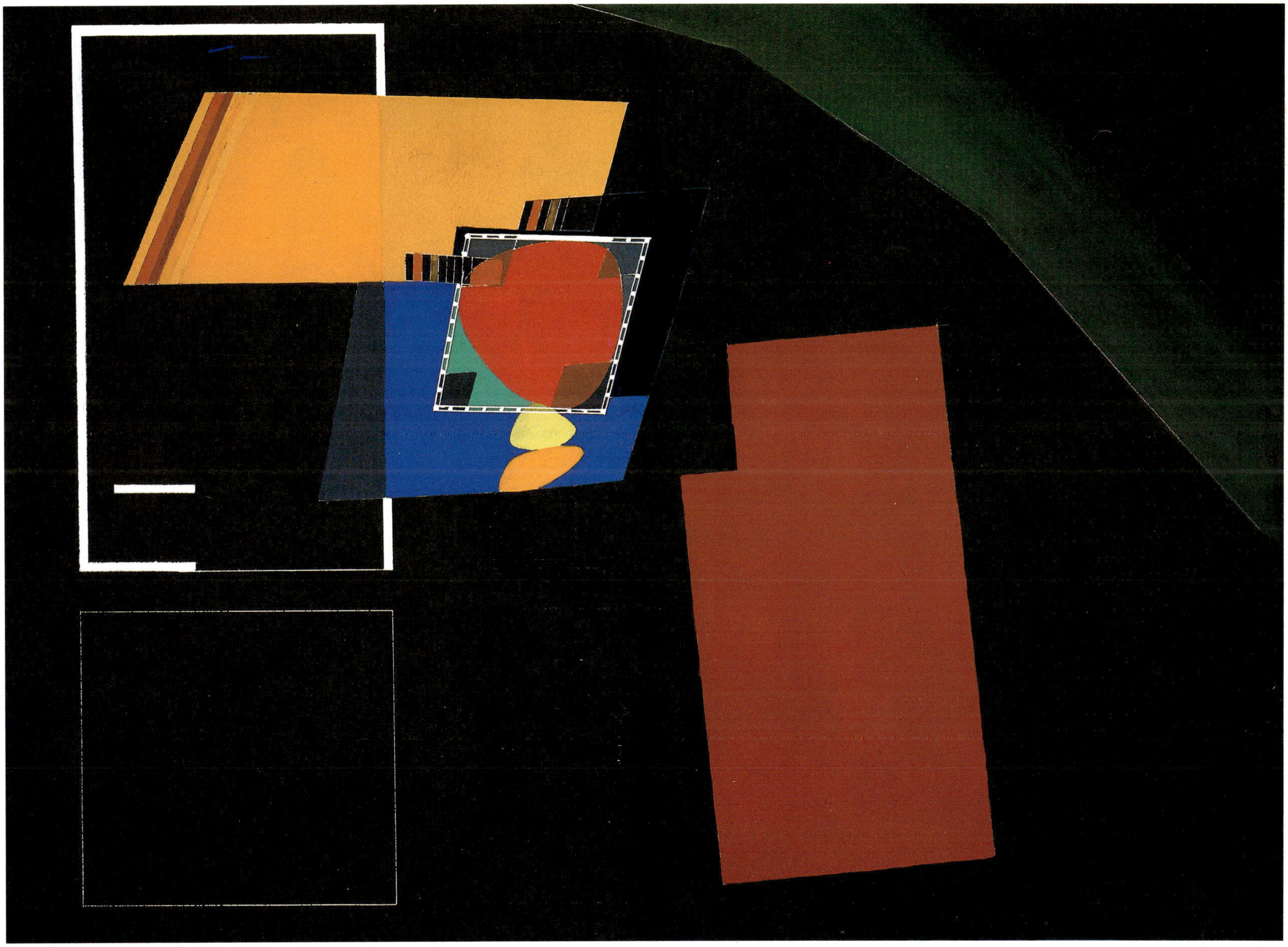

4, 5. »Paintings« des Turmes, Frühjahr 1992.

4, 5. »Paintings« of the tower, spring 1992.

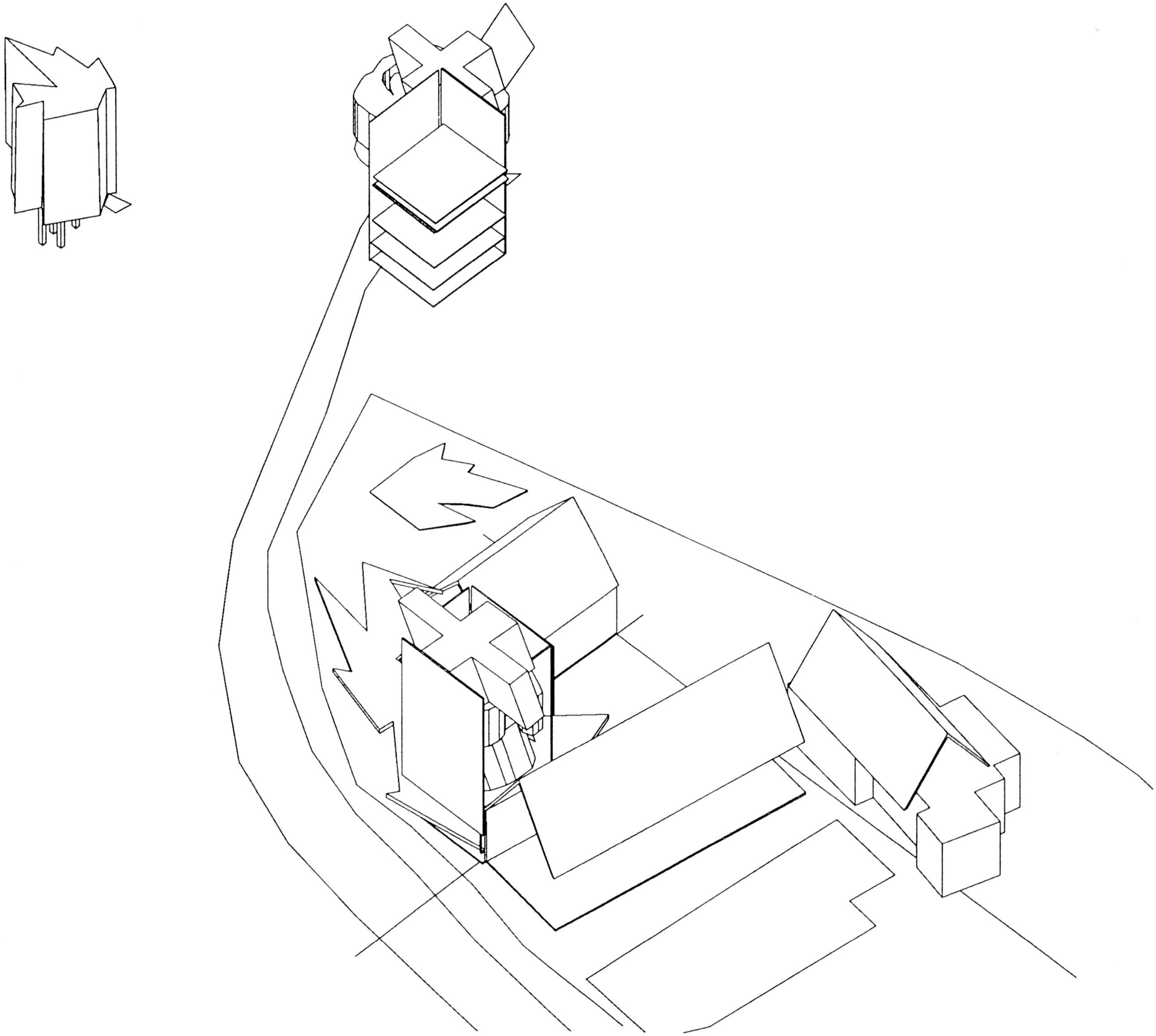

6. Axonometrie des Turmes, Frühjahr 1992.
7. Perspektive des Turmes, Frühjahr 1992.

6. Axonometric view of the tower, spring 1992.
7. Perspective view of the tower, spring 1992.

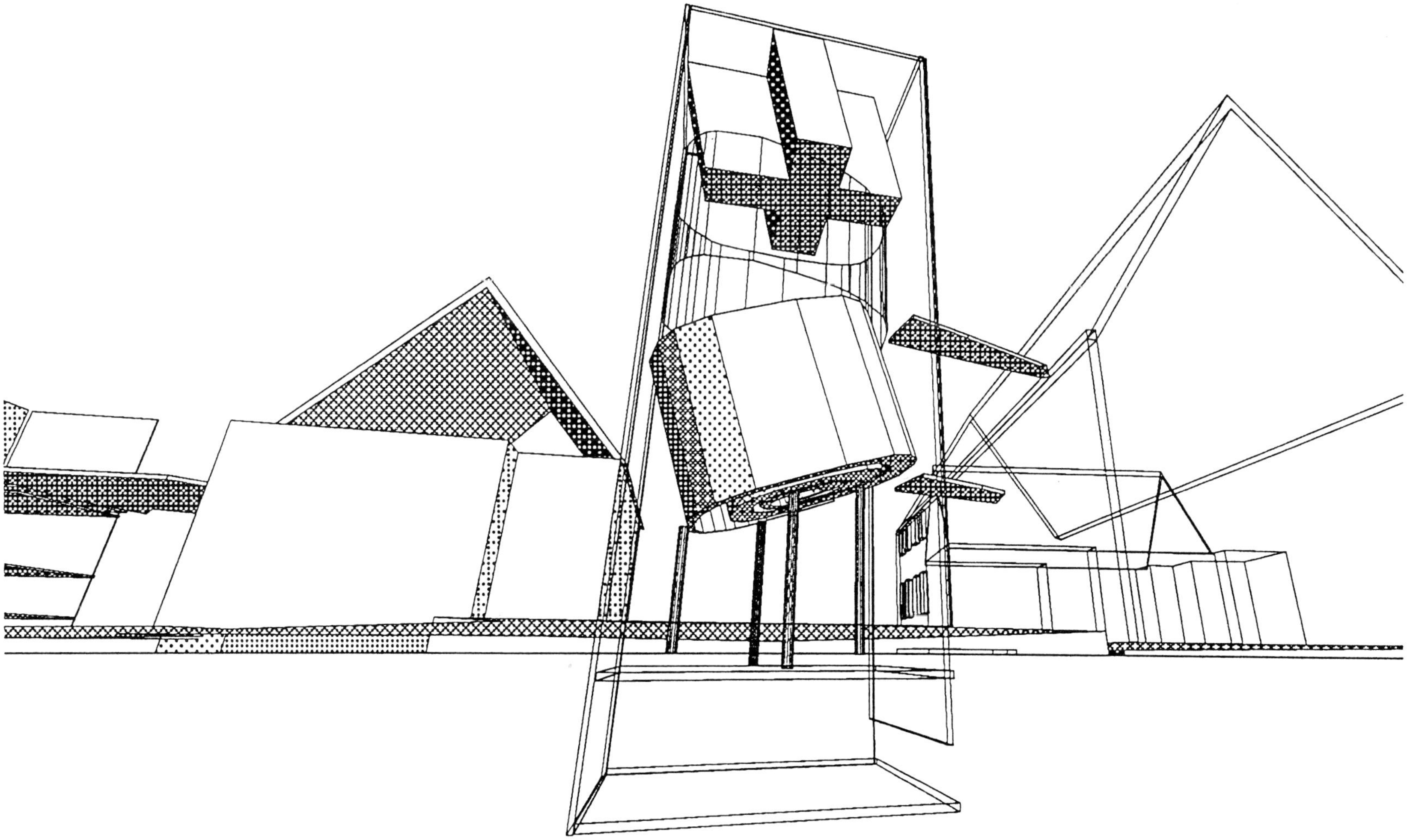

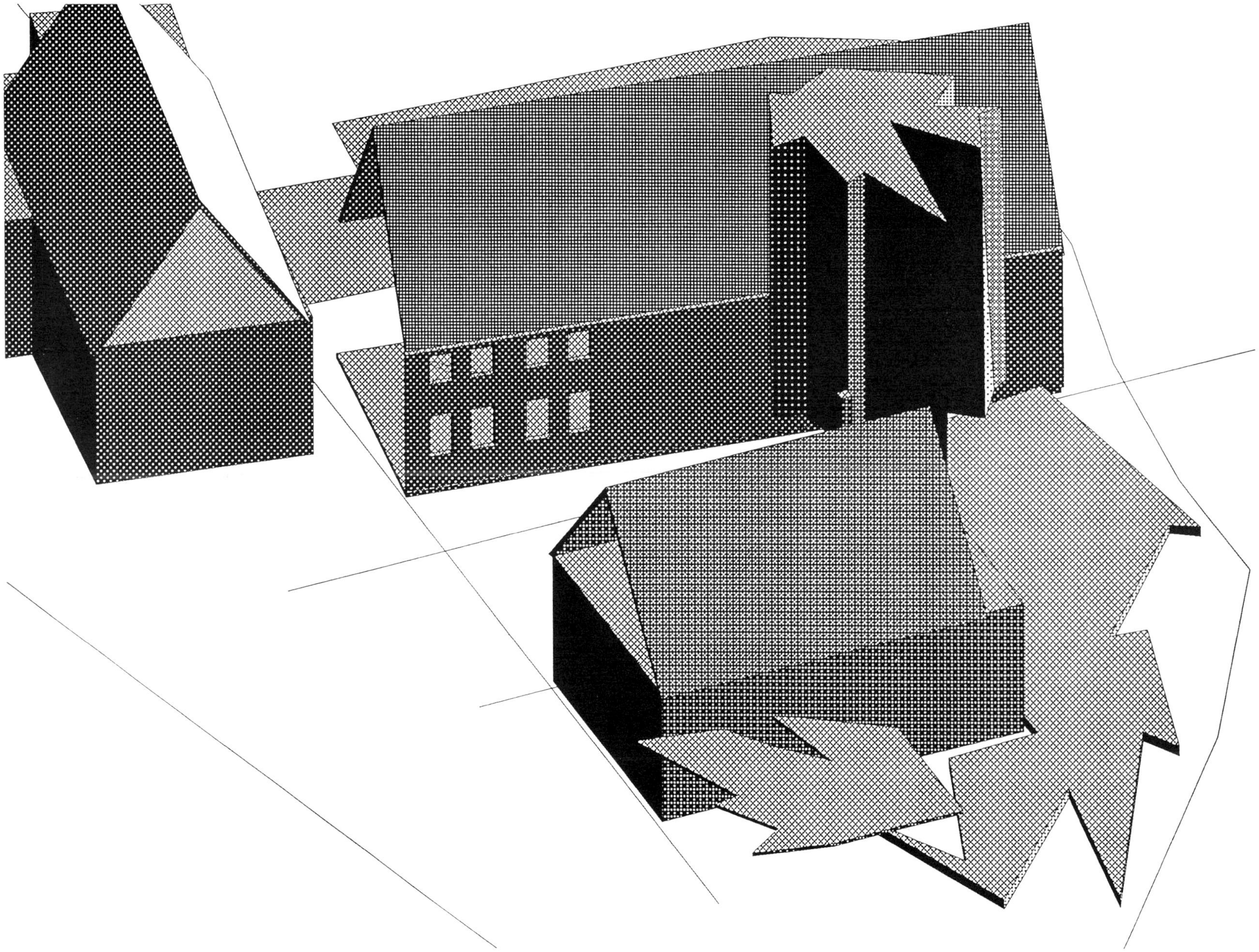

8. Axonometrie des Turmes, Frühjahr 1992.
9. Perspektive des Turmes, Frühjahr 1992.

8. Axonometric view of the tower, spring 1992.
9. Perspective view of the tower, spring 1992.

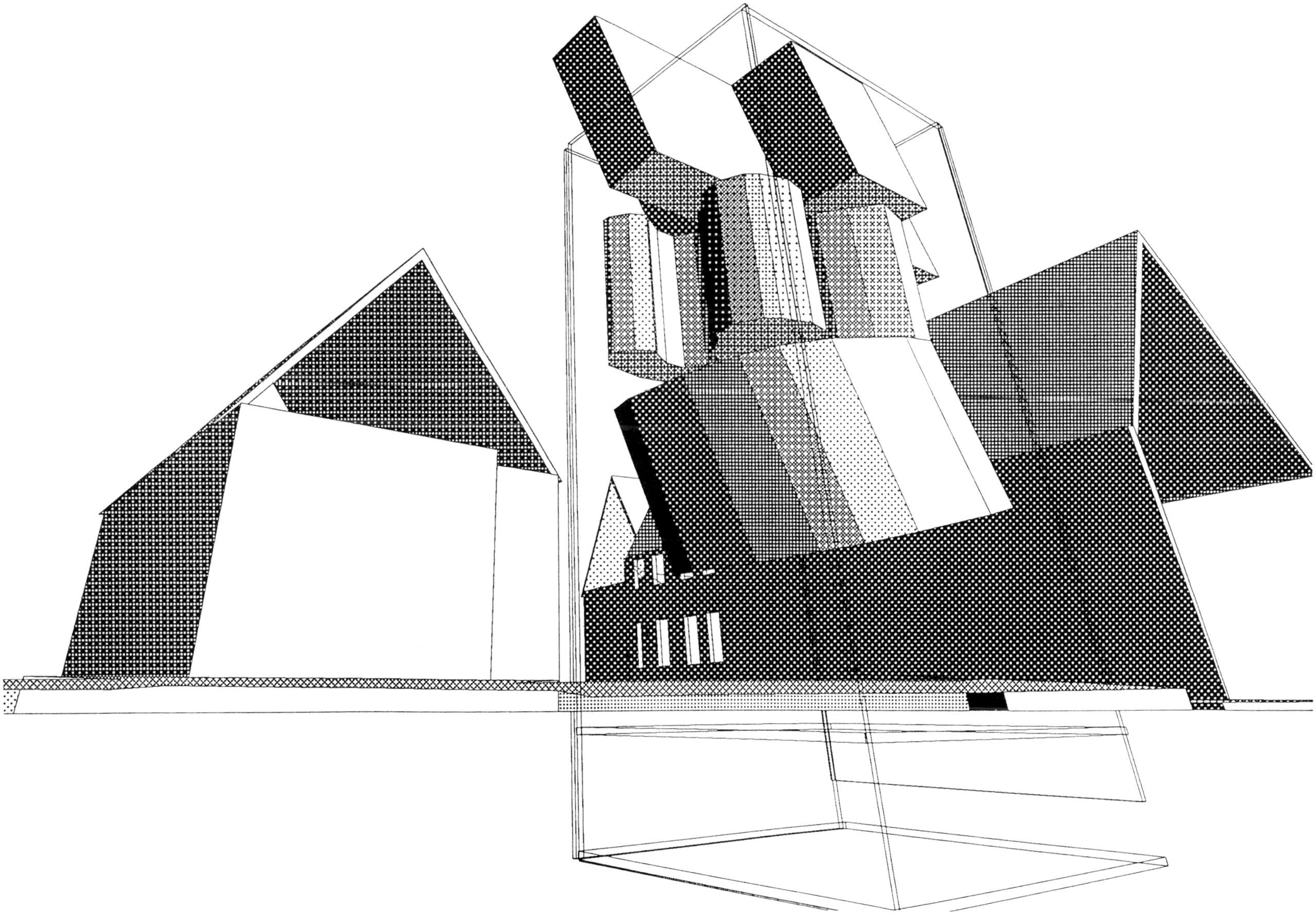

10,11. Modell, Frühjahr 1993.

10,11. Model, spring 1993.

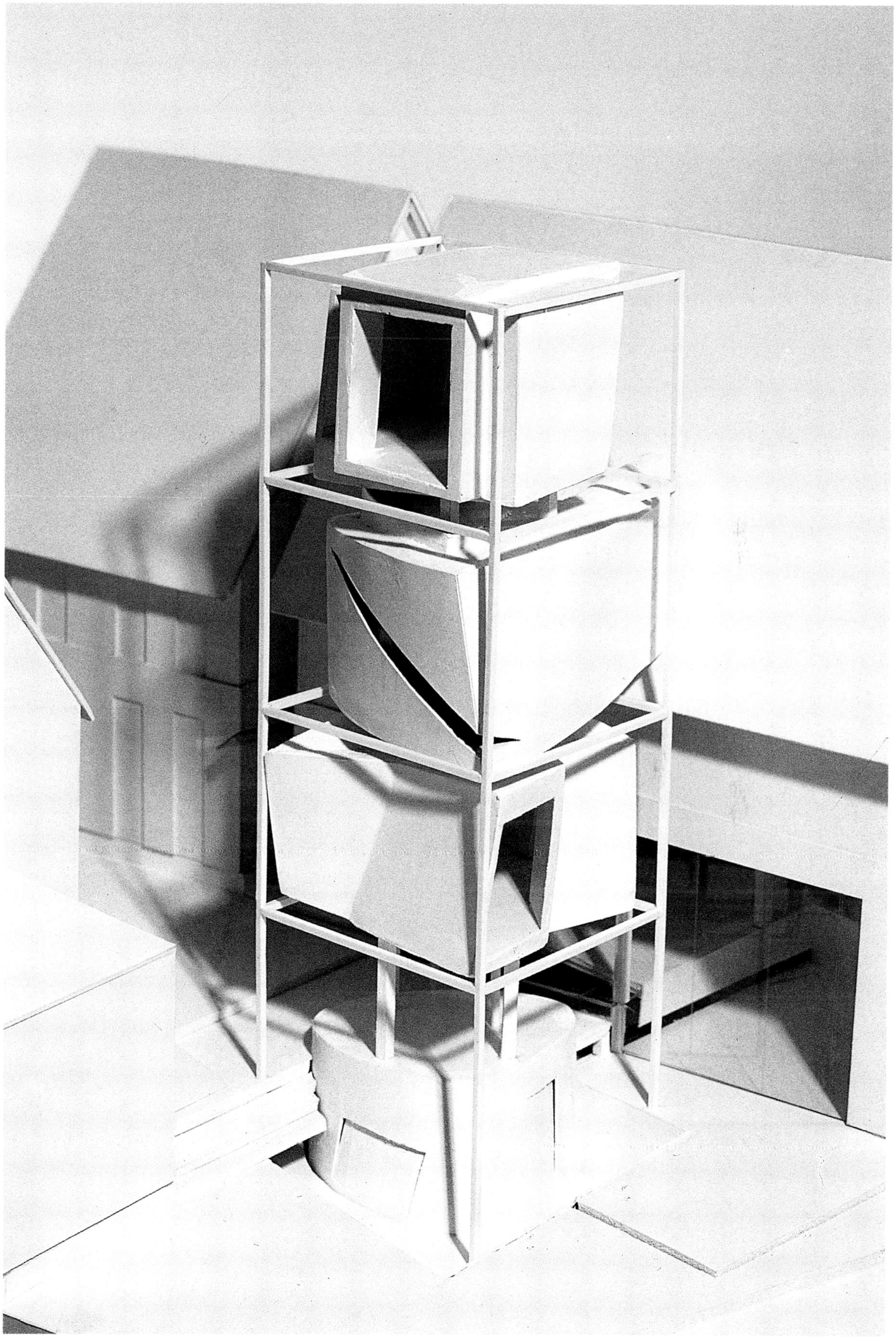

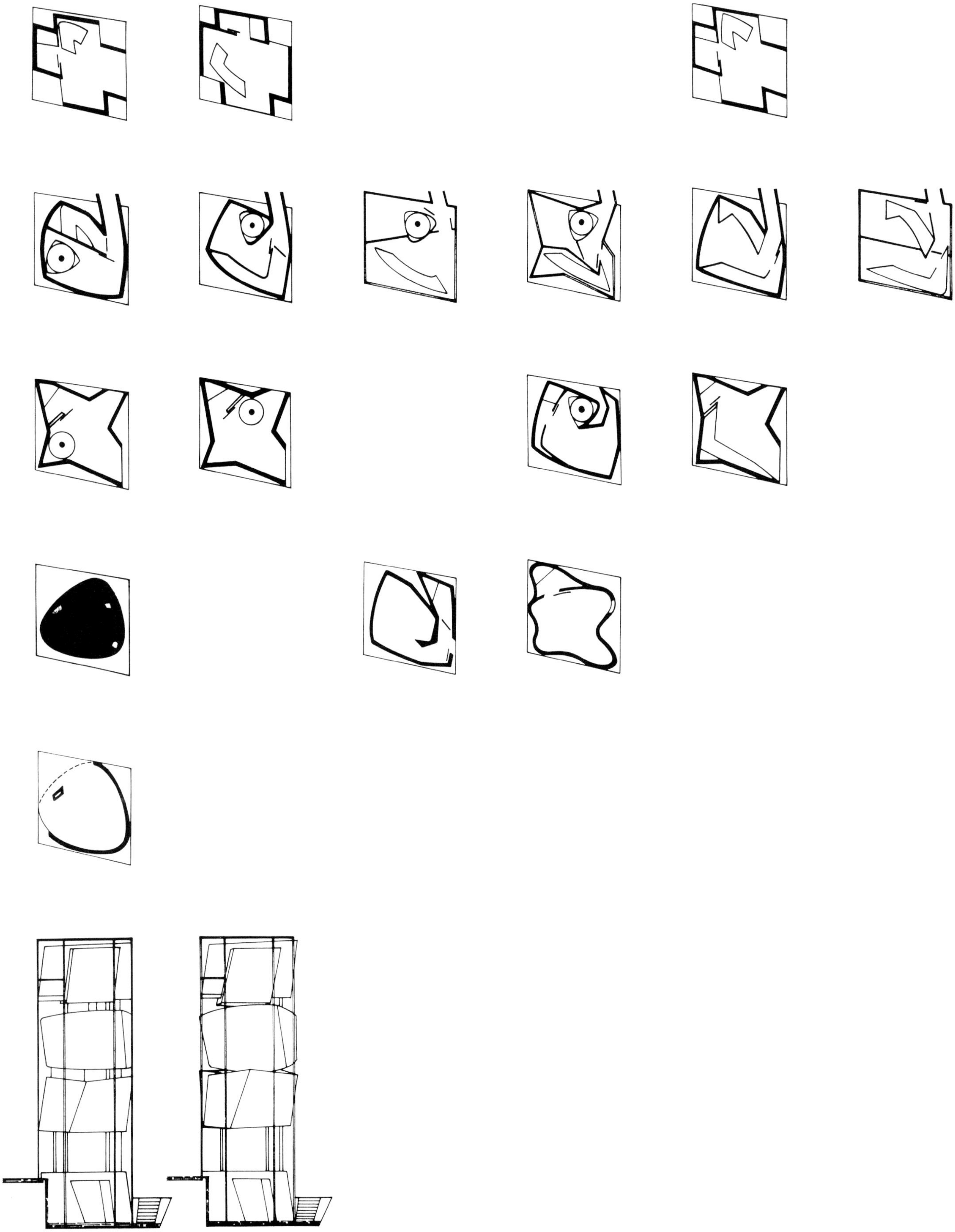

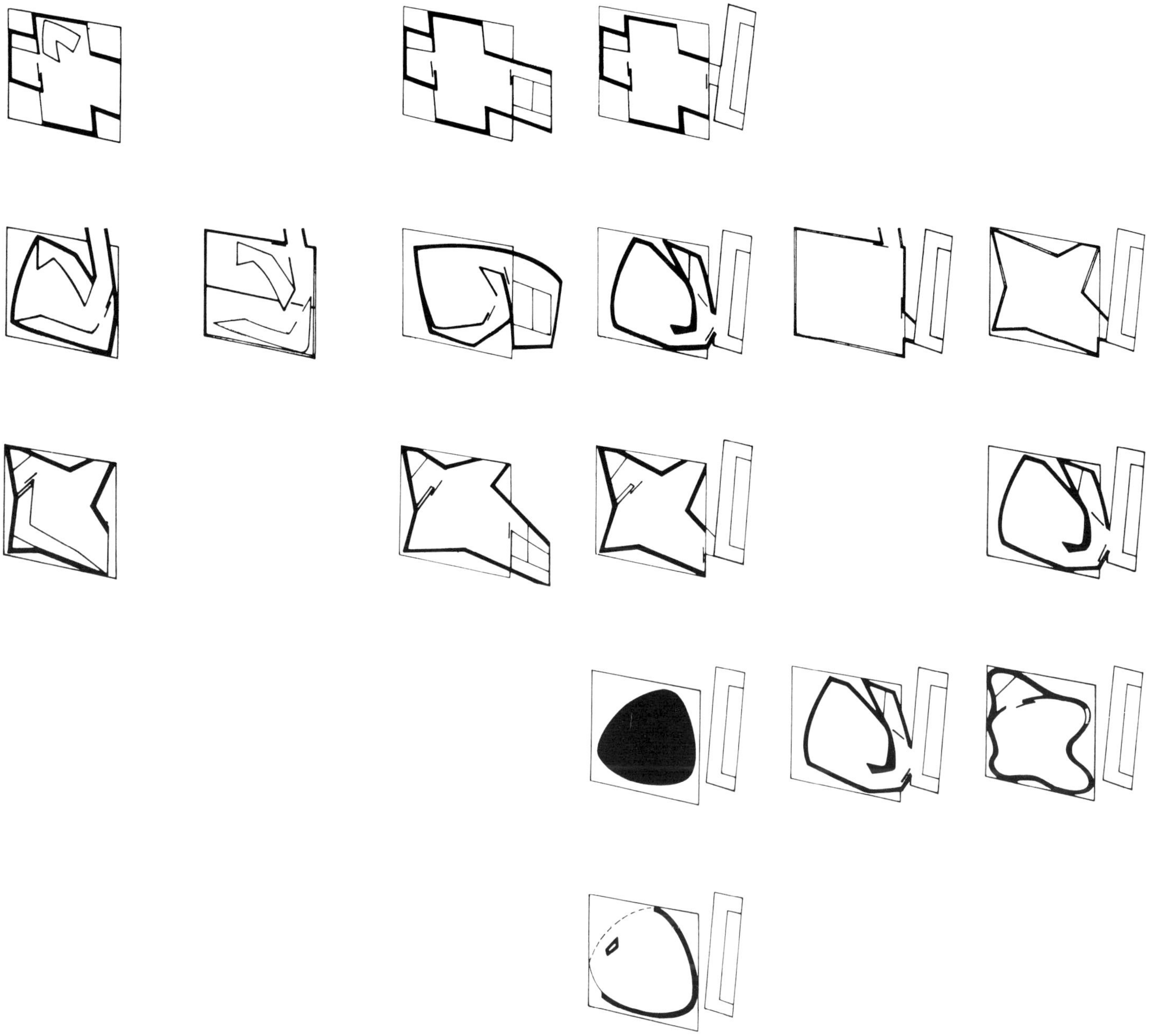

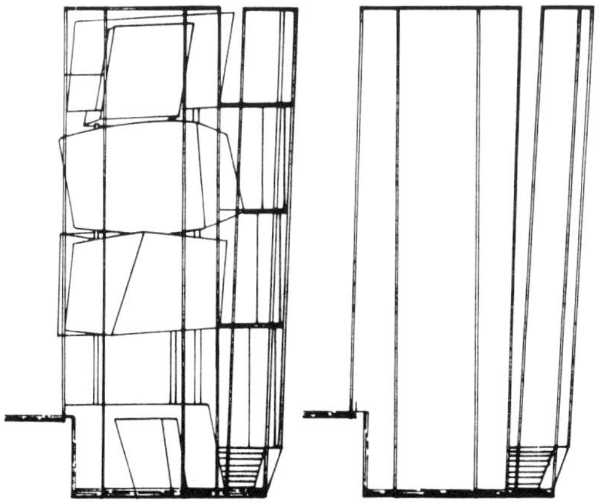

12, 13. Typologische Studien zum Turm, Sommer 1992.

12, 13. Typological studies for the tower, summer 1992.

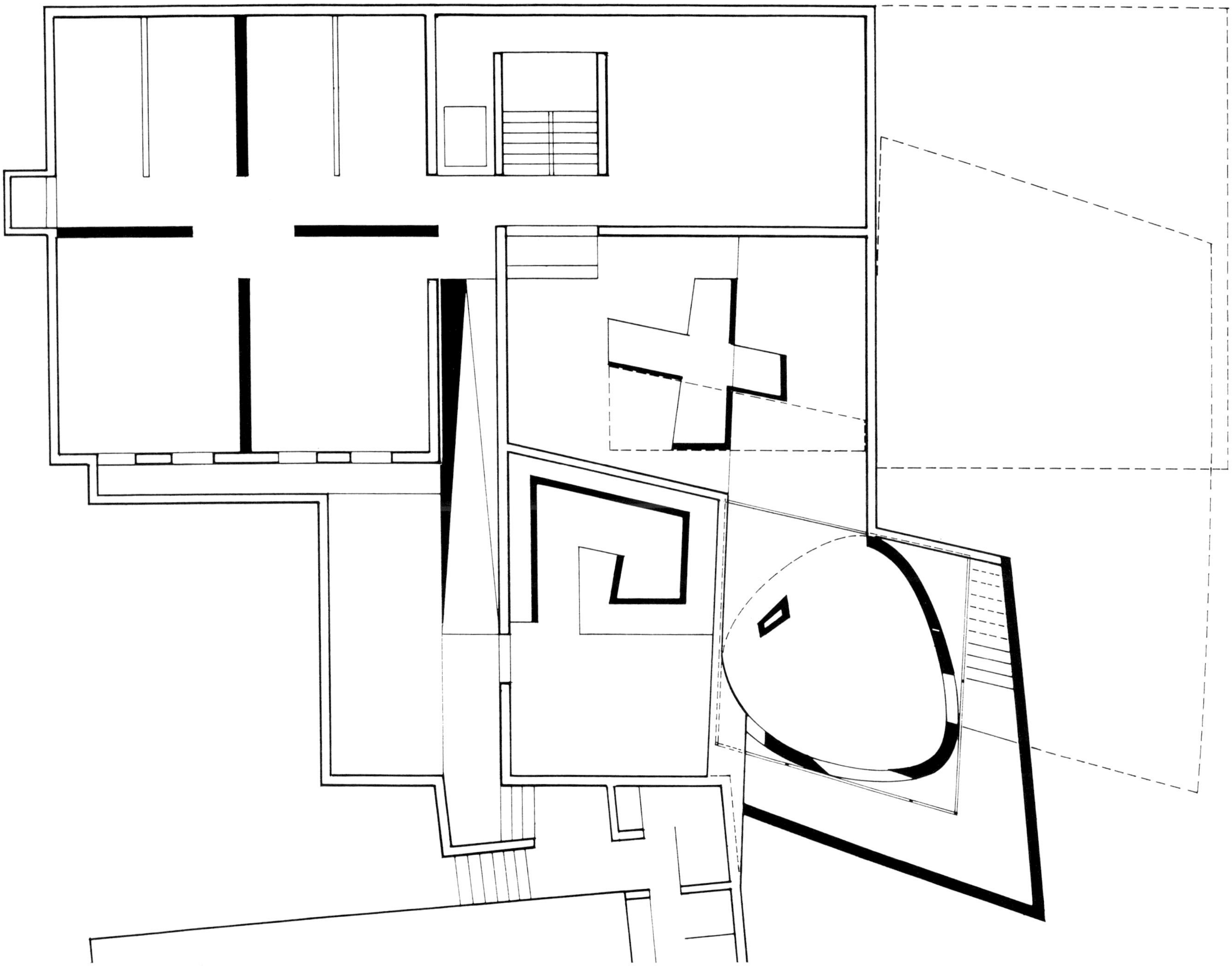

14. Grundriß des Untergeschosses, Sommer 1992.
15. Grundriß des Erdgeschosses, Sommer 1992.

14. Plan of the basement, summer 1992.
15. Plan of the ground floor, summer 1992.

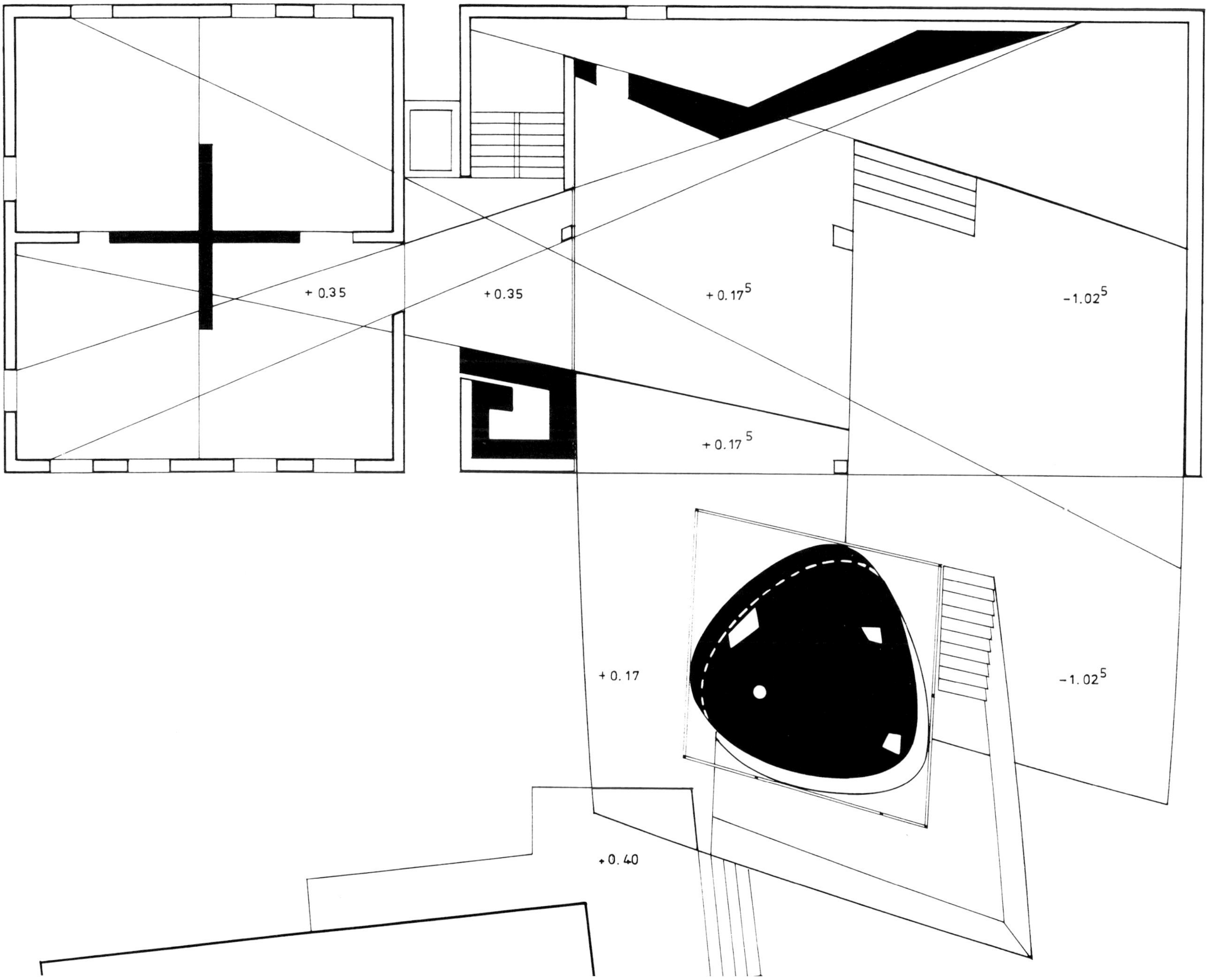

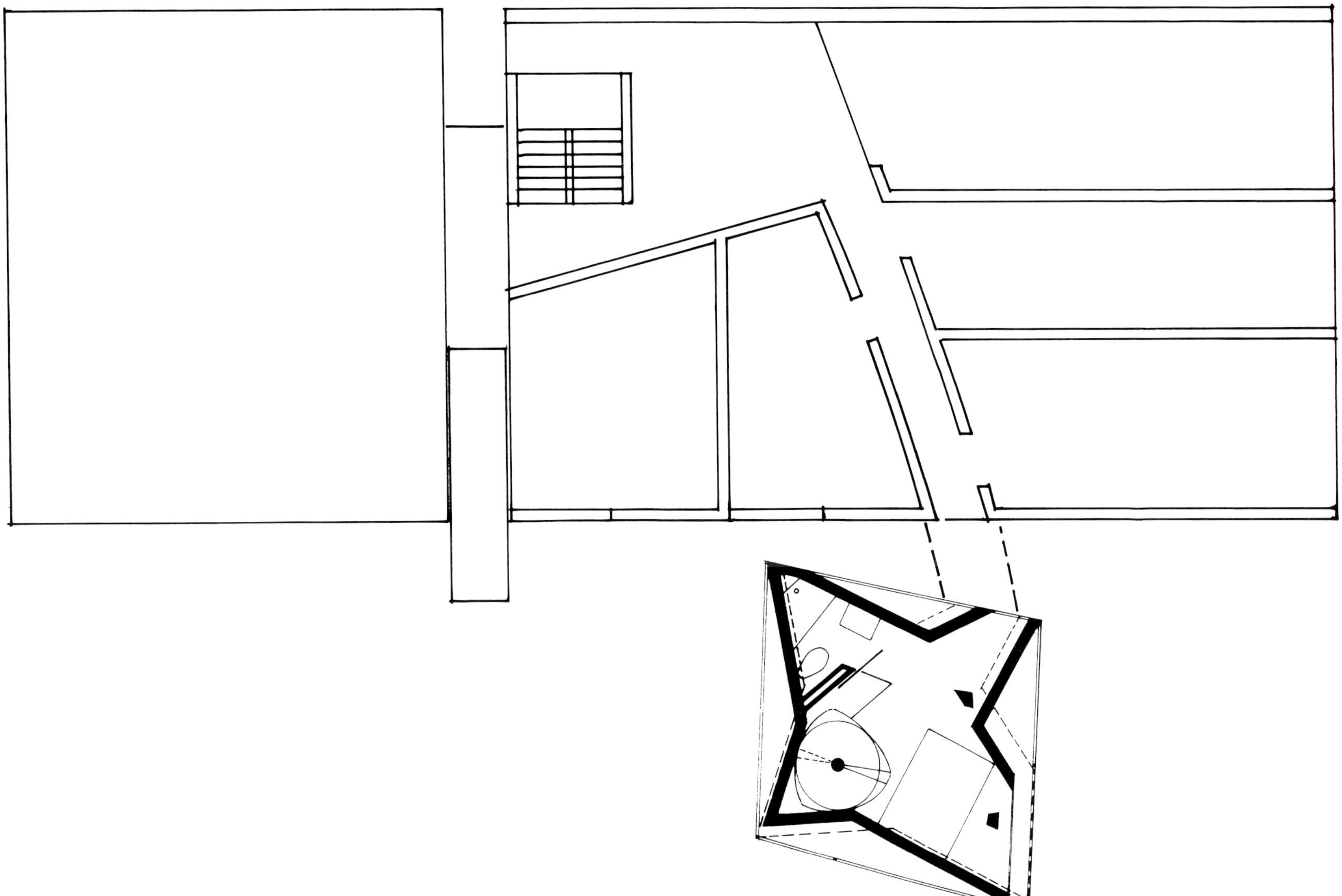

16. Grundriß des 1. Obergeschosses, Sommer 1992.
17. Grundriß des 2. Obergeschosses, Sommer 1992.

16. Plan of the 1st floor, summer 1992.
17. Plan of the 2nd floor, summer 1992.

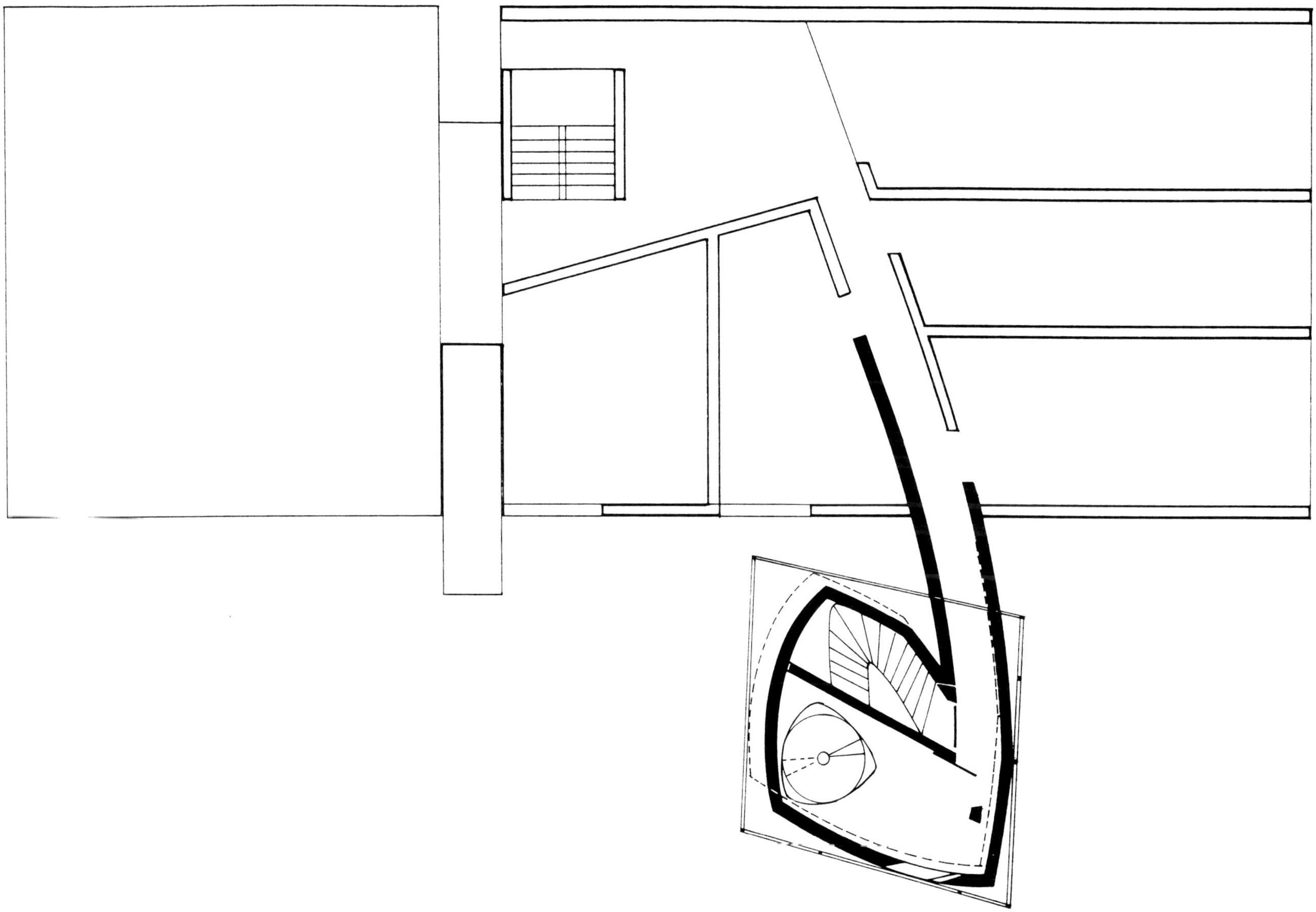

18. Grundriß des 3. Obergeschosses, Sommer 1992.
19. Schnitt durch den Turm, Sommer 1992.

18. Plan of the 3rd floor, summer 1992.
19. Section through the tower, summer 1992.

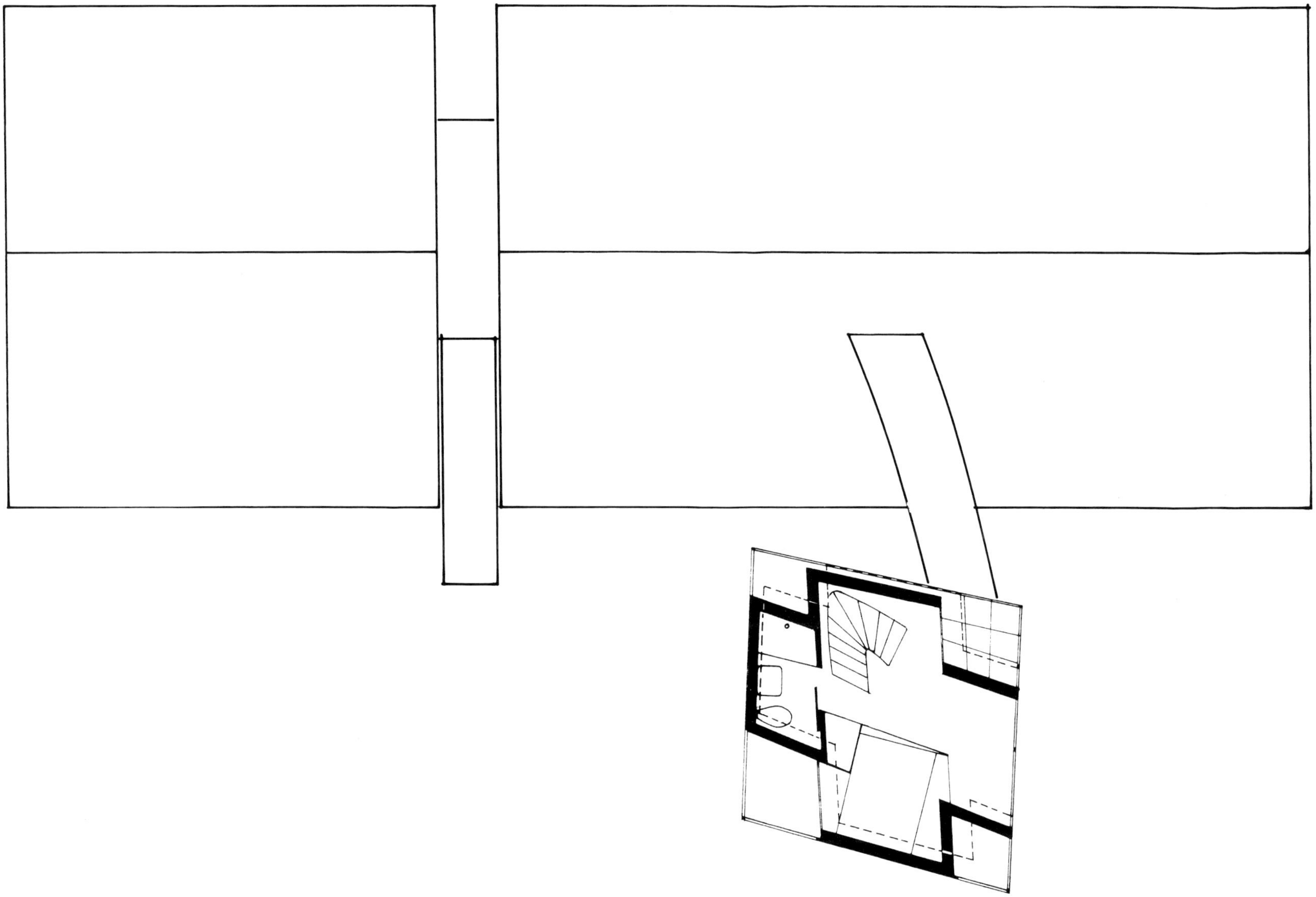

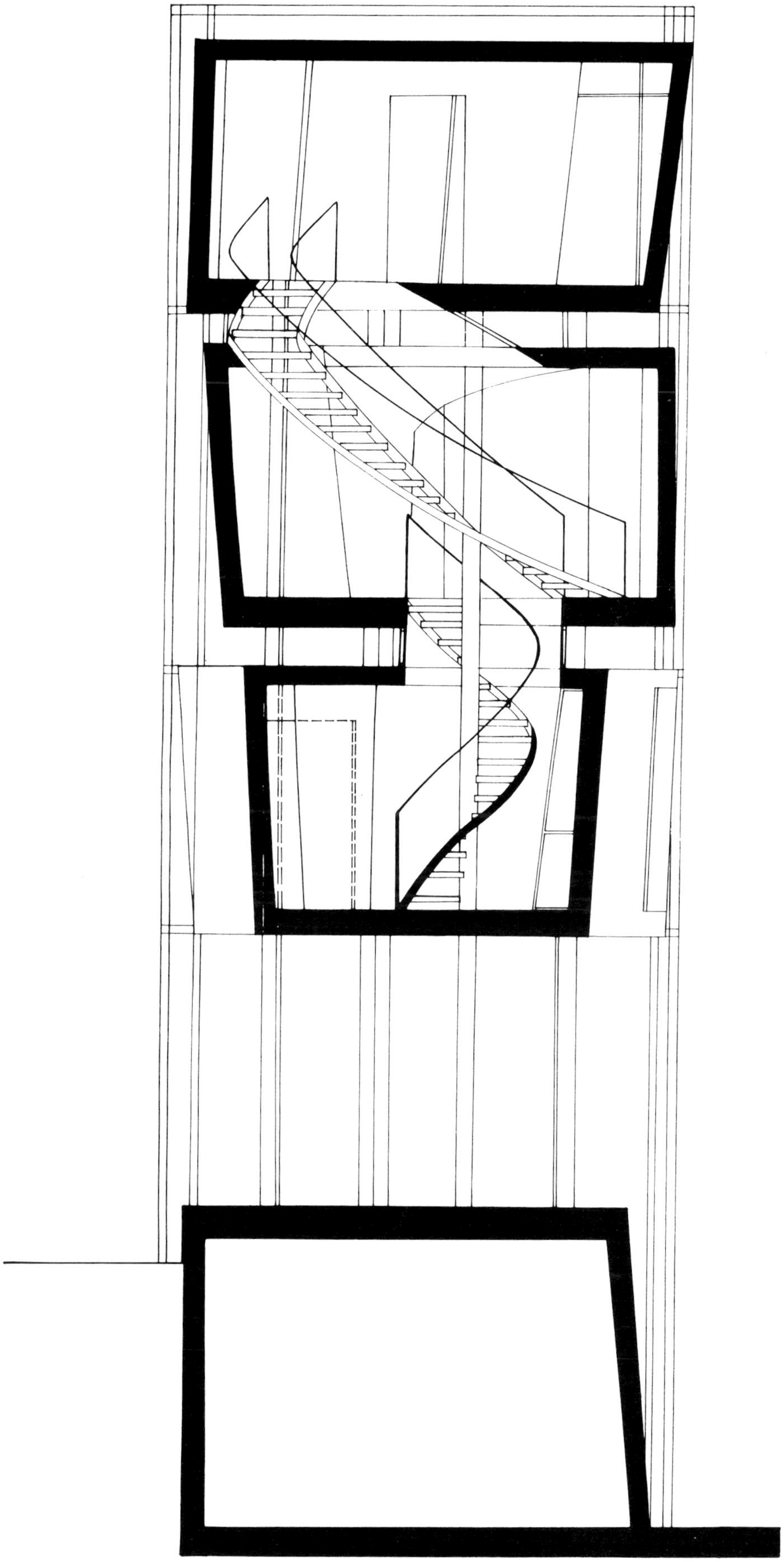

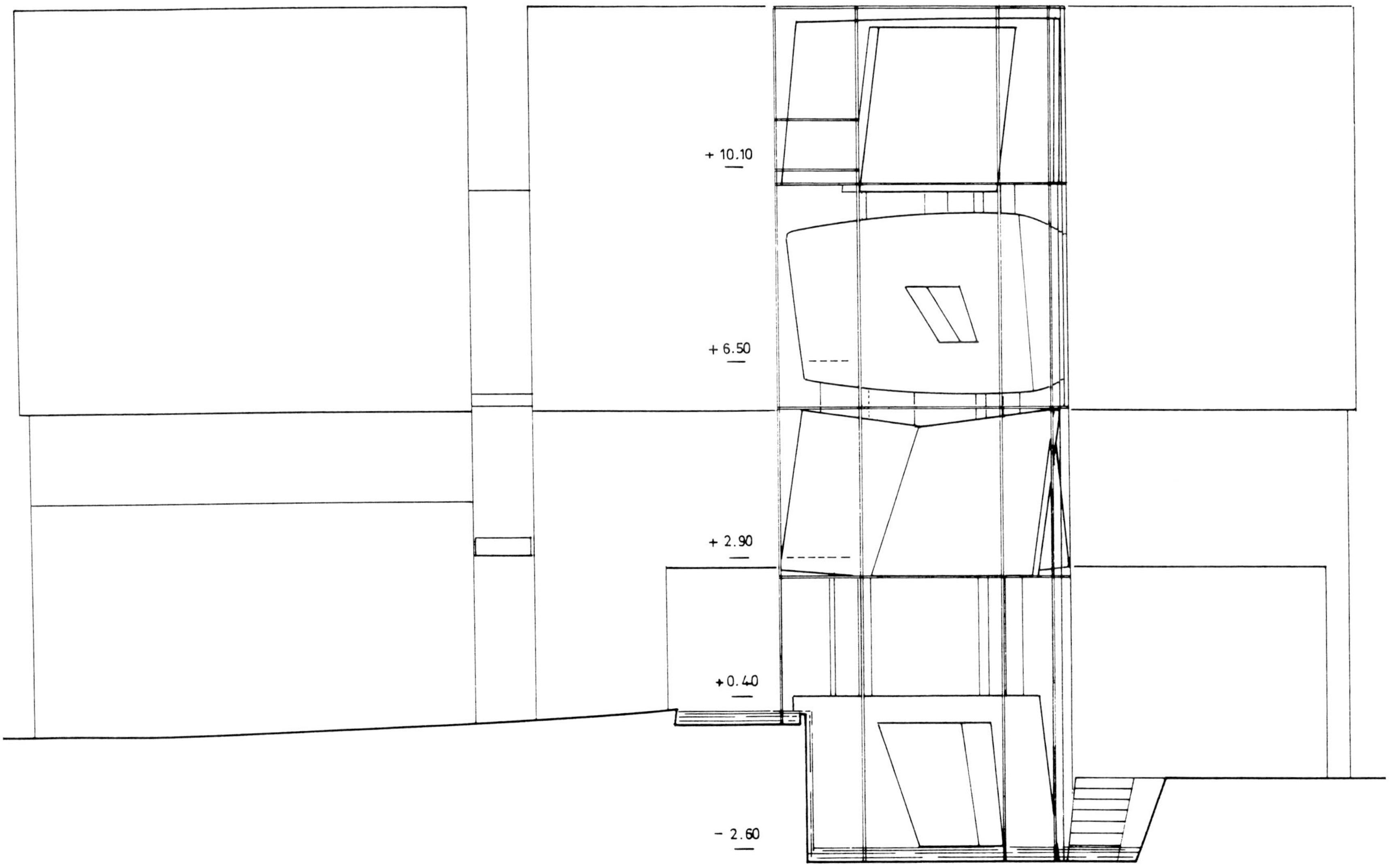
+ 10.10
+ 6.50
+ 2.90
+ 0.40
- 2.60

20. Aufriß von Westen, Sommer 1992.
21. Aufriß von Süden, Sommer 1992.

20. Elevation from the west, summer 1992.
21. Elevation from the south, summer 1992.

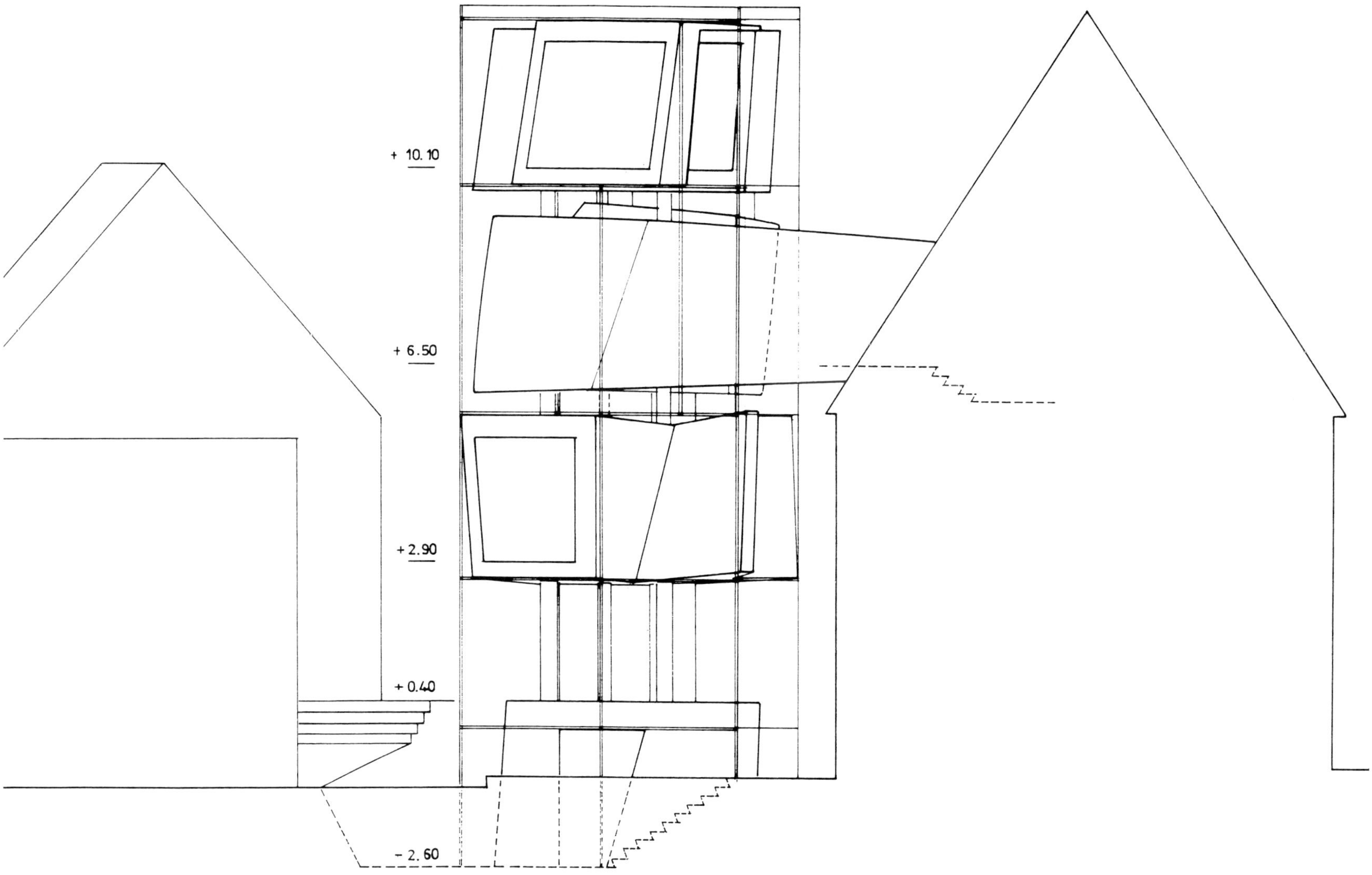

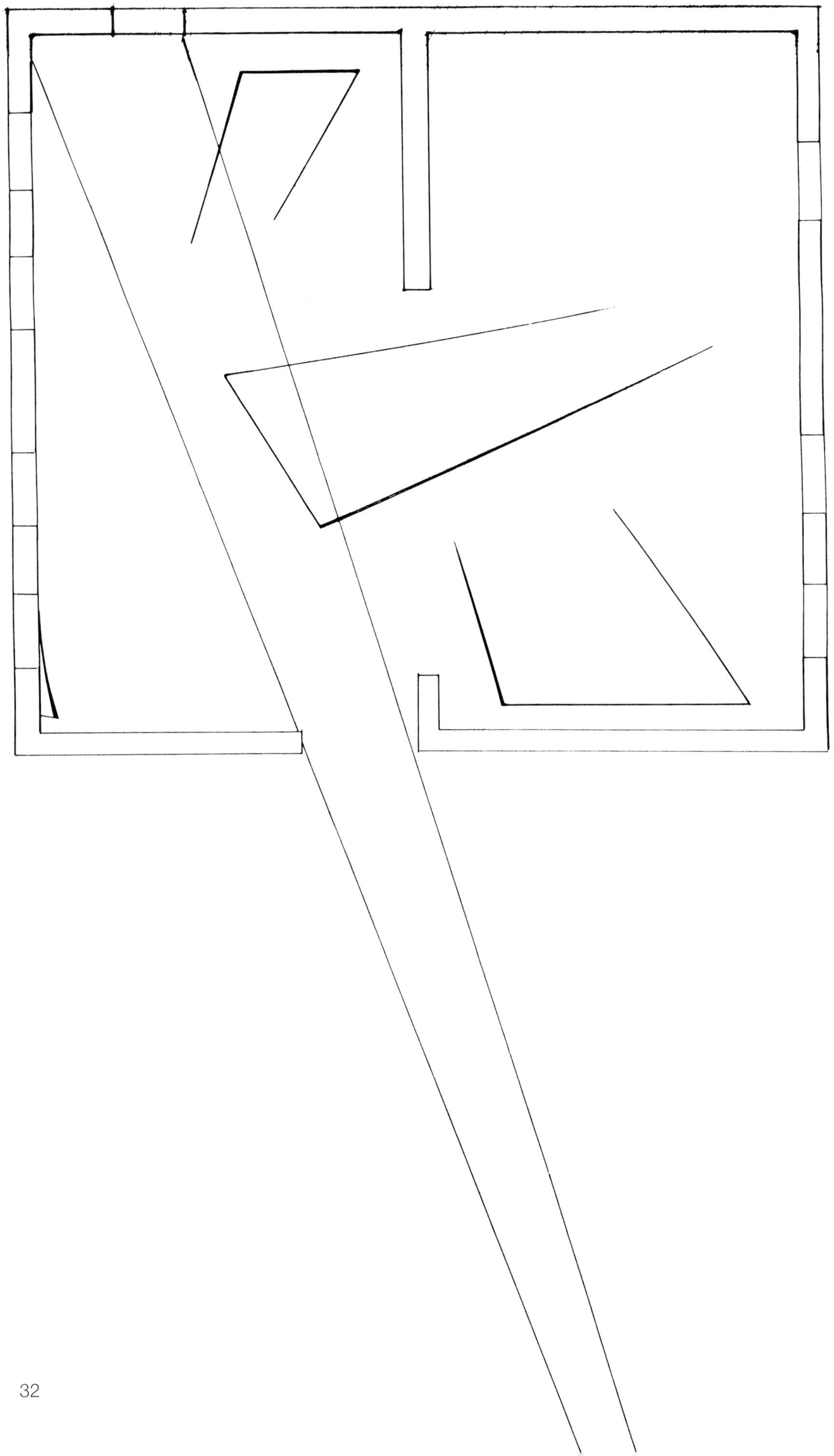

22. Deckenspiegel der Halle im Erdgeschoß, Frühjahr 1993.
23. Grundriß der Halle im Erdgeschoß und Aufriß des Raumteilers in der Halle, Frühjahr 1993.

22. Reflective ceiling of the hall on the ground floor, spring 1993.
23. Floor plan of the hall on the ground floor and elevation of the room division in the hall, spring 1993.

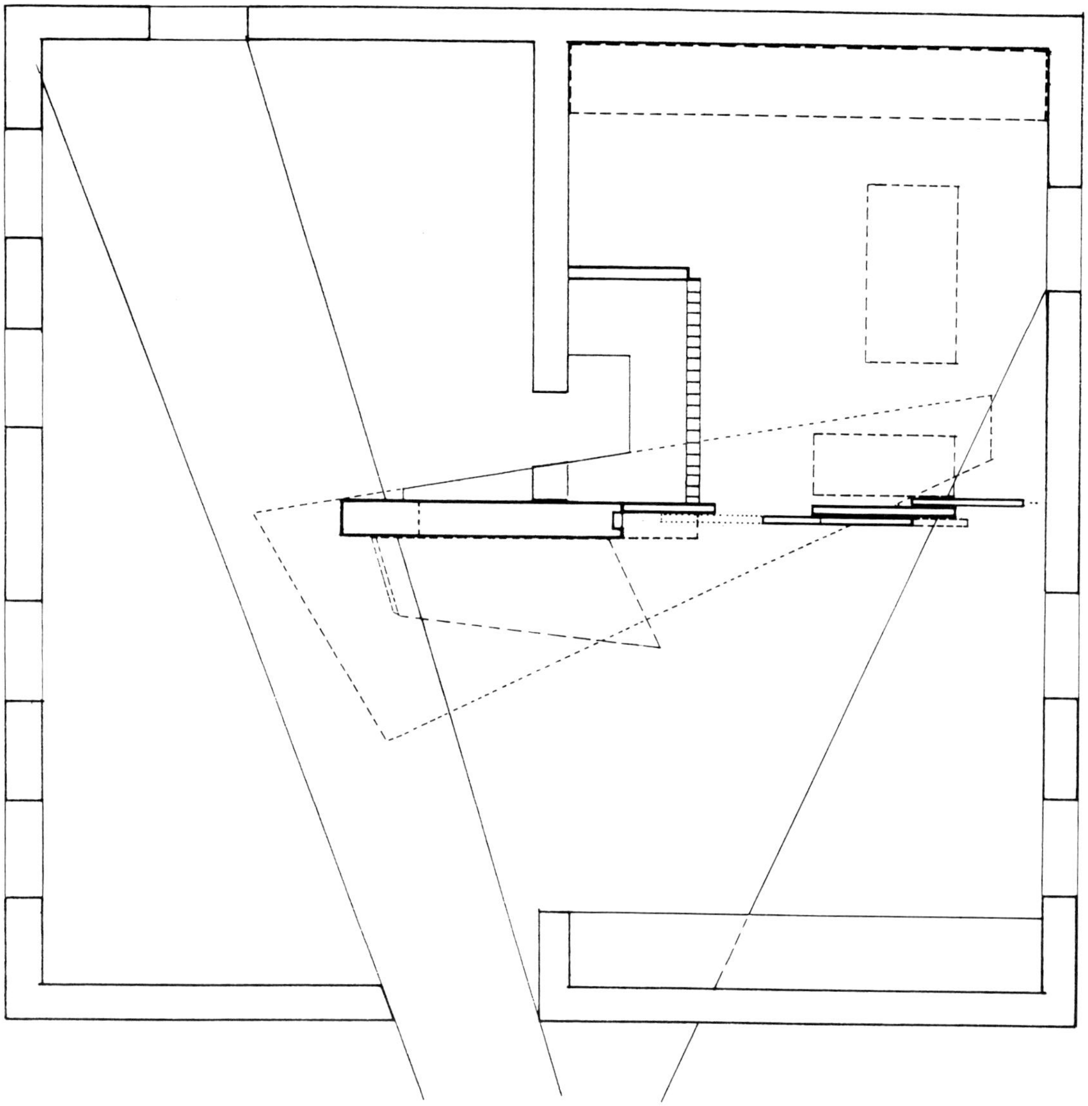

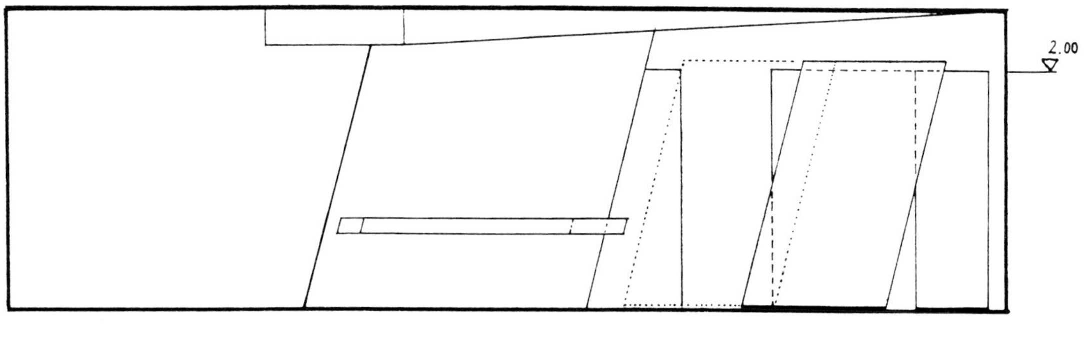

S. 34/35
24. Perspektive der Halle im Erdgeschoß, Frühjahr 1993.

p. 34/35
24. Perspective view of the hall on the ground floor, spring 1993.

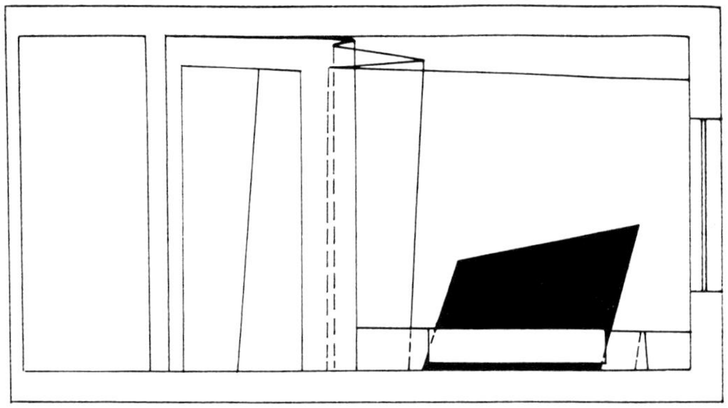

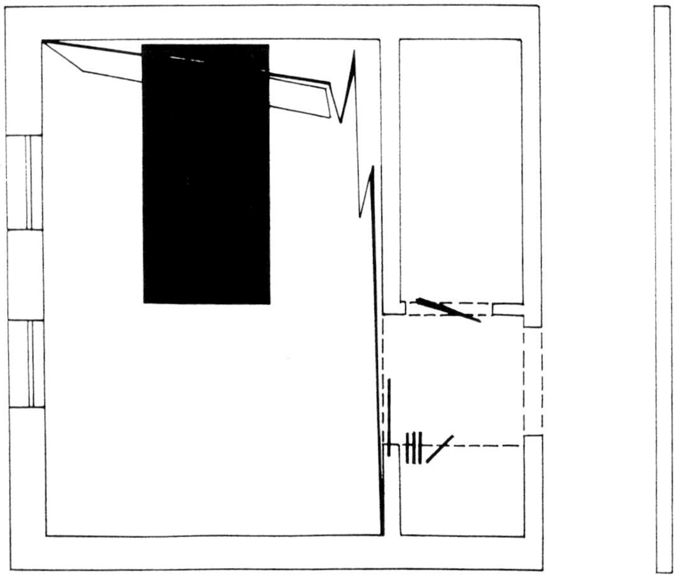

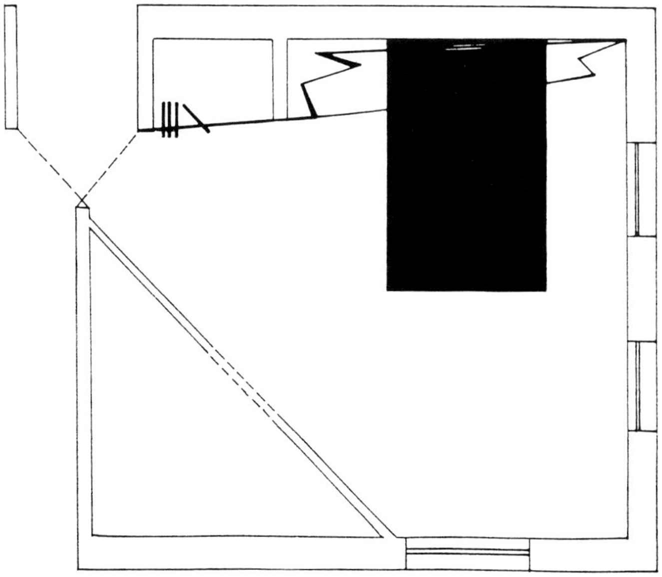

25, 26. Grund- und Aufrisse von Gästezimmern
im 1. Obergeschoß, Frühjahr 1993.
25, 26. Floor plans and elevations of guest rooms
on the 1st floor, spring 1993.

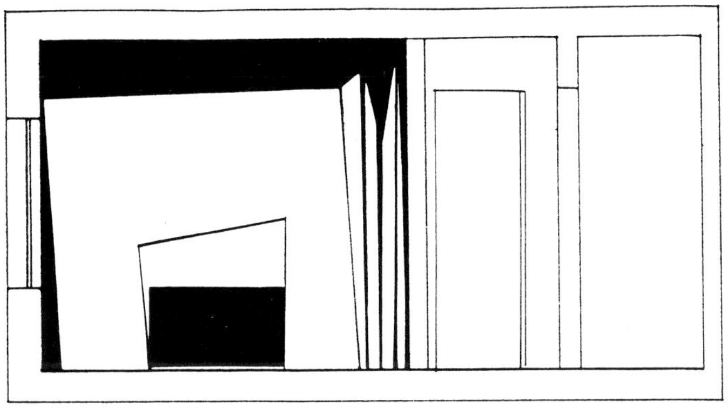

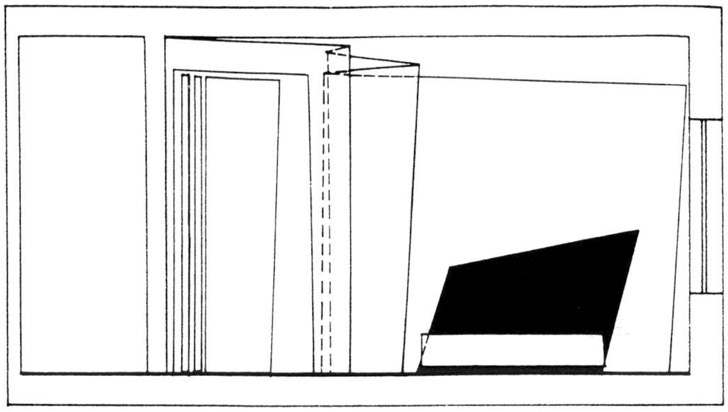

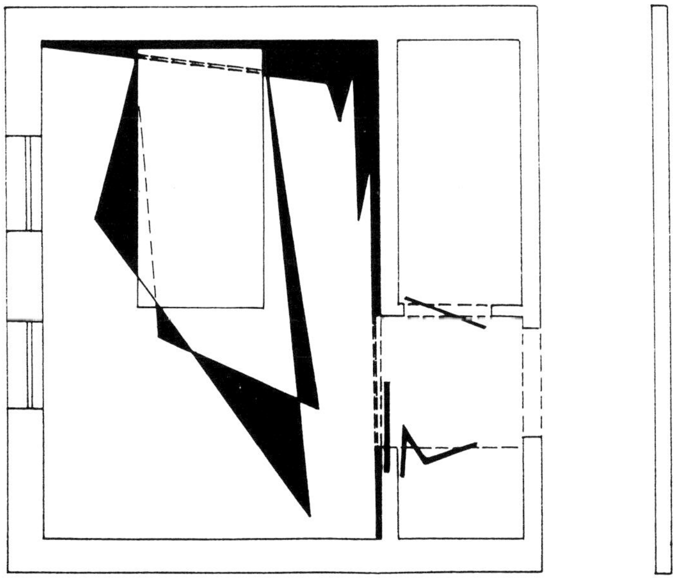

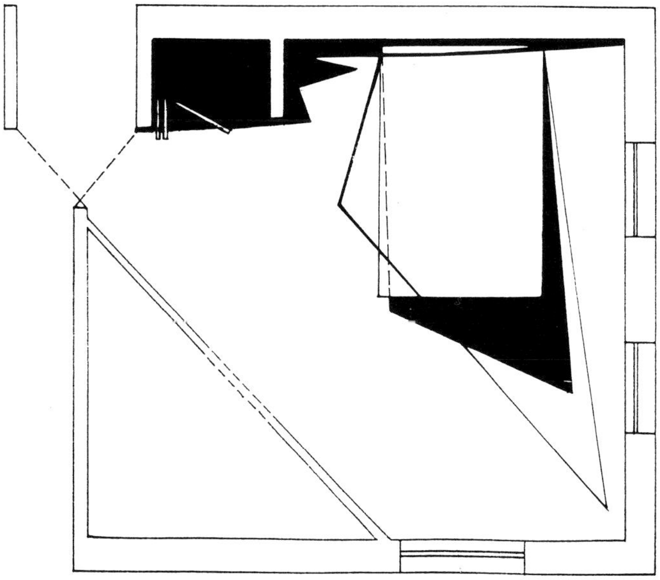

27. Grund- und Aufrisse von Gästezimmern im 1. Obergeschoß, Frühjahr 1993.
28. Aufrisse eines Gästezimmers im 3. Obergeschoß und des Flurs im 1. Obergeschoß, Frühjahr 1993.

27. Floor plans and elevations of guest rooms on the 1st floor, spring 1993.
28. Elevations of a guest room on the 3rd floor and of the corridor on the 1st floor, spring 1993.

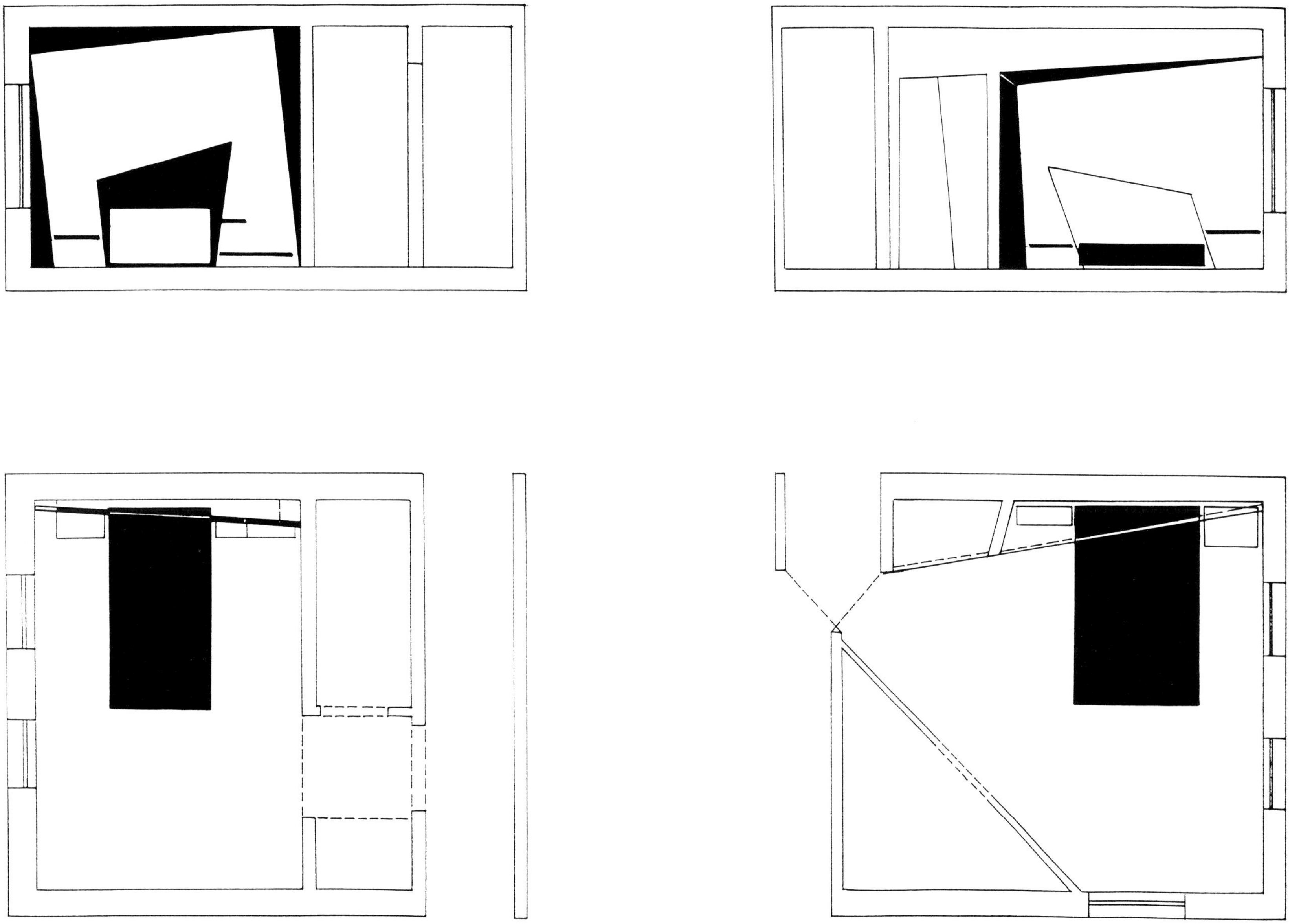

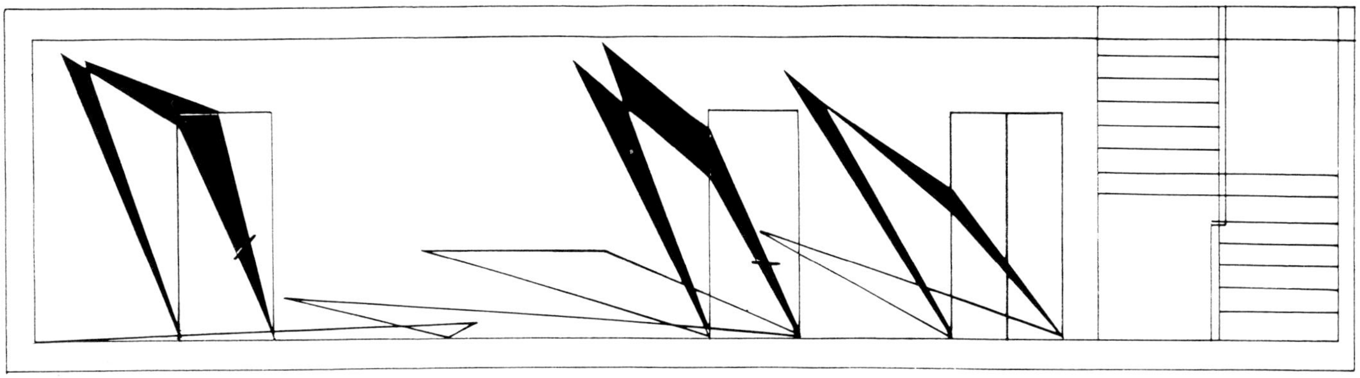

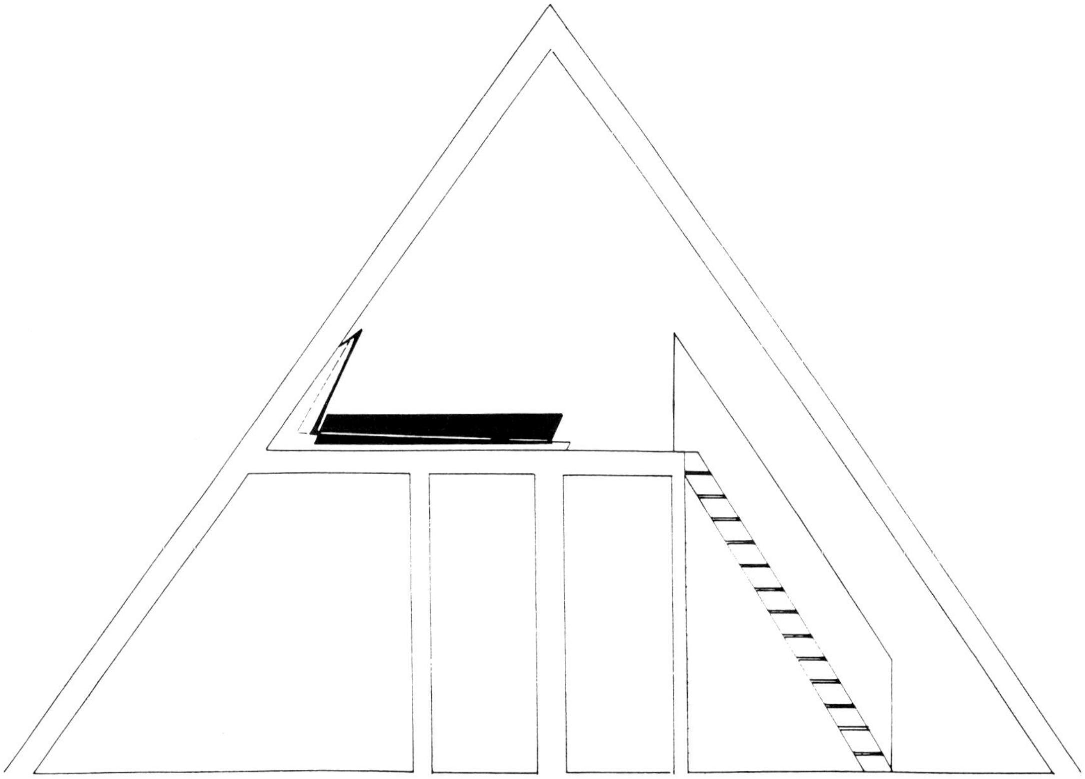

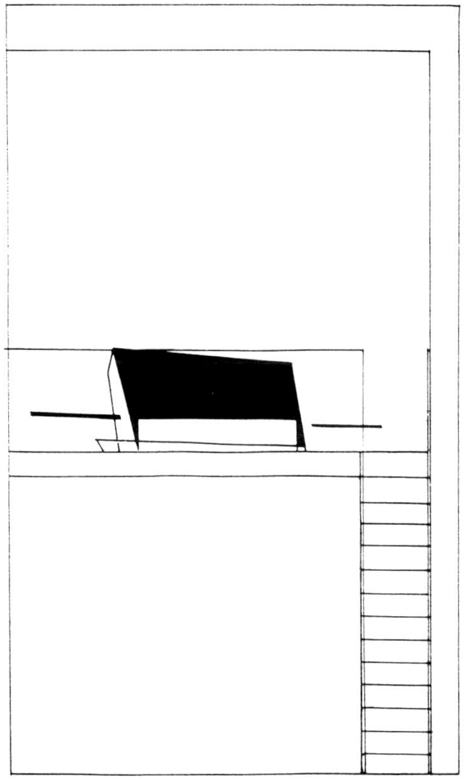

29. Deckenspiegel des »Blobby« im Unterge-
schoß, Frühjahr 1993.
30. Deckenspiegel der »Blobby« im Untergeschoß,
Sommer 1993.

29. Reflective ceiling of the »blobby« in the base-
ment, spring 1993.
30. Reflective ceiling of the »blobby« in the base-
ment, summer 1993.

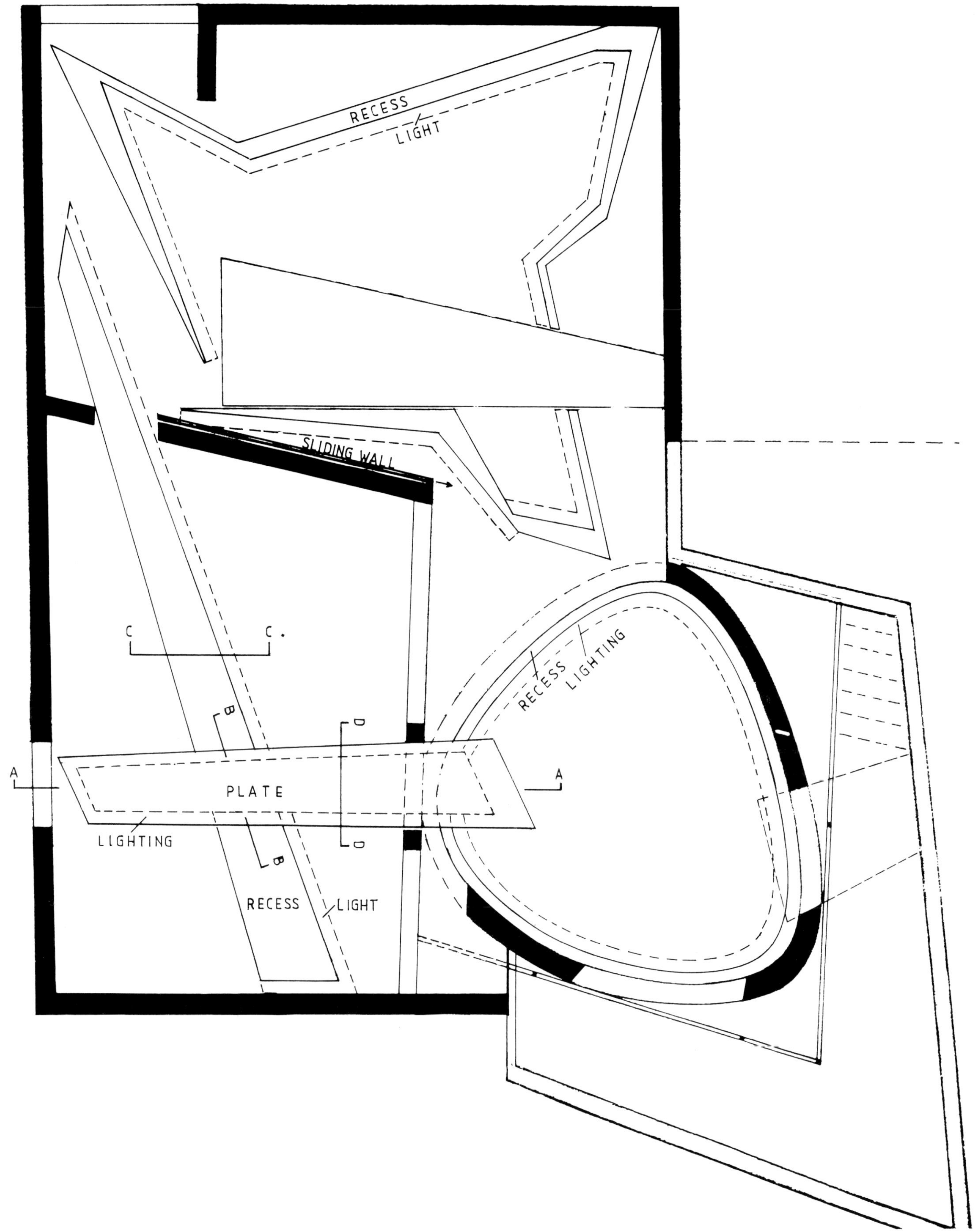
RECESS
LIGHT
SLIDING WALL
C
C
RECESS
LIGHTING
B
D
A
PLATE
A
LIGHTING
D
B
RECESS
LIGHT

31, 32. Details der Decke des »Blobby« im Untergeschoß.

31, 32. Details of the ceiling of the »blobby« in the basement.

33, 34. Halle im Erdgeschoß.
35, 36. Treppenhaus.
37, 38. Der »blobby« im Untergeschoß.
39, 40. Gästezimmer »Lampo-Flash« im 2. Obergeschoß.
41. Gästezimmer »Lampo-Flash« im 3. Obergeschoß.
42. Flur im 2. Obergeschoß.
43, 44. Gästezimmer »Ellipse« im 2. Obergeschoß.
45. Flur im 1. Obergeschoß.
46. Gästezimmer »Mistero« im 1. Obergeschoß.
47. Gästezimmer »Trapez« im 1. Obergeschoß.

33, 34. Hall on the 1st floor.
35, 36. Staircase.
37, 38. The »blobby« in the basement.
39, 40. Guest room »Lampo-Flash« on the 2nd floor.
41. Guest room »Lampo-Flash« on the 3rd floor.
42. Corridor in the 2nd floor.
43, 44. Guest room »Ellipse« on the 2nd floor.
45. Corridor on the 1st floor.
46. Guest room »Mistero« on the 1st floor.

Zaha Hadid mit Billie Strauß in der Galerie Billie Strauß, Stuttgart, 1991.

Zaha Hadid with Billie Strauß in the Galerie Billie Strauß, Stuttgart, 1991.

Biographie von Zaha Hadid

1950 in Bagdad geboren
1971 Bachelor of Science in Mathematik an der American University in Beirut
1972–77 Studium an der Architectural Association School of Architecture in London
1977 Mitglied des Office for Metropolitan Architectural (OMA) und Beginn der Lehre an der Architural Association School of Architecture (mit Rem Koolhaas und Elia Zenghelis)
1980–87 Leiterin eines Fachbereichs der Architectural Association School of Architecture
1982 Goldmedaille für ihren Entwurf für 59 Eaton Place, London
1982 Erster Preis im »Peak Competition«, Hongkong
1986 Lehre an der Graduate School of Design der Harvard University, Cambridge, MA
1987 Gastprofessur an der Graduate School of Architecture, Planning and Preservation der Columbia University, New York
1993 Lehre an der Graduate School of Architecture, Planning and Preservation der Columbia University
1994 Lehre am Kenzo-Tange-Lehrstuhl der Graduate School of Design der Harvard University

Biography of Zaha Hadid

1950 Born in Baghdad
1971 Bachelor of Science in mathematics at the American University in Beirut
1972–77 Studied at the Architectural Association School of Architecture in London
1977 Member of the Office for Metropolitan Architecture. Started teaching at the Architectural Association School of Architecture (with Rem Koolhaas and Elia Zenghelis)
1980–87 Head of a department at the Architectural Association School of Architecture
1982 Gold medal for her project for 59 Eaton Place, London
1982 First prize in the »Peak Competition«, Hong Kong
1986 Taught at the Graduate School of Design, Harvard University, Cambridge, MA
1987 Guest professor at the Graduate School of Architecture, Planning and Preservation, Columbia University, New York
1993 Taught at the Graduate School of Architecture, Planning and Preservation, Columbia University
1994 Taught at the Kenzo Tange Chair, Graduate School of Design, Harvard University

Werke von Zaha Hadid (Auswahl)

Erweiterung des Parlamentsgebäudes in Den Haag, 1978/79, Projekt.
Residenz des irischen Premierministers in Dublin, 1979/80, Projekt.
Penthouse 59 Eaton Place, London, 1981/82, Projekt.
La Villette, Paris, 1982/83, Projekt.
The Peak, Hongkong, 1982/83, Projekt.
Innenraumgestaltung Halkin Place, London, 1984, Projekt.
Trafalgar Square, London, 1985, Projekt.
Innenraumgestaltung der HTV Studios, London, 1985, Projekt.
Melbury Court, London, 1985, Projekt.
New National Theater, Tokio, 1985, Projekt.
Inneneinrichtung für W. Bitar, 24 Cathcart Road, London, 1986.
Hamburger Hafen, 1986, Projekt.
Bürogebäude am Kurfürstendamm, Berlin, 1986, Projekt.
Wohngebäude in Berlin-Kreuzberg, 1986-93.
Möbel für Edra, Pisa, 1987.
Geschirr für Swid Powell, New York, 1987.
West Hollywood Civic Center, 1987, Projekt.
Al Wahda Sports Stadium, Abu Dhabi, 1988, Projekt.
Victoria-Areal, Berlin, 1988, Projekt.
Feuerwehrgebäude für Vitra, Weil am Rhein, 1989 bis 1993.
Hafenstraße, Hamburg, 1989, Projekt.
Osaka Folly, Osaka, Japan, 1989, Projekt.
Media Park, Düsseldorf, 1989, Projekt.
Moon Soon Restaurant, Sapporo, Japan, 1989/90.
Leicester Square, London, 1990. Projekt.
Video-Pavillon in Groningen, Niederlande, 1990.
Hotel und Wohnkomplex in Abu Dhabi, 1990. Projekt.
Plan für Berlin, 1990, Projekt.
Rheinauhafen, Köln, 1992, Projekt.
Erweiterung des Arthotels Billie Strauß, Kirchheim-Nabern, 1992, Projekt.
Gestaltung der Ausstellung »The Great Utopia«, Solomon R. Guggenheim Museum, New York, 1992/93.
Konzerthalle in Kopenhagen, 1993, Projekt.
Französisches Gymnasium, London, 1994, Projekt.
Opernhaus in Cardiff, England, 1994, Projekt.

Works by Zaha Hadid (selection)

Extension to the parliament building in The Hague, 1979/80, project.
Residence of the Irish Prime Minister in Dublin, 1979/80, project.
Penthouse 59 Eaton Place, London, 1981/82, project.
La Villette, Paris, 1982/83, project.
The Peak, Hong Kong, 1982/83, project.
Interior design for Halkin Place, London, 1984, project.
Trafalgar Square, London, 1985, project.
Interior design for HTV Studios, London, 1985, project.
Melbury Court, London, 1985, project.
New National Theater, Tokyo, 1985, project.
Interior design for W. Bitar, 24 Cathcart Road, London, 1986.
Hamburg Harbour, 1986, project.
Office building in the Kurfürstendamm, Berlin, 1986, project.
Apartment building in Berlin-Kreuzberg, 1986 to 1993.
Furniture for Edra, Pisa, 1987.
Plates for Swid Powell, New York, 1987.
West Hollywood Civic Center, 1987, project.
Al Wahda Sports Stadium, Abu Dhabi, 1988, project.
Victoria area, Berlin, 1988, project.
Fire Station for Vitra, Weil am Rhein, 1989-93.
Hafenstraße, Hamburg, 1989, project.
Osaka Folly, Osaka, Japan, 1989, project.
Media Park, Düsseldorf, 1989, project.
Moon Soon Restaurant, Sapporo, Japan, 1989/90.
Leicester Square, London, 1990. project.
Video pavilion in Groningen, Netherlands, 1990.
Hotel and residential complex in Abu Dhabi, 1990, project.
Plan for Berlin, 1990, project.
Rheinauhafen, Cologne, 1992, project.
Extension to the Arthotel Billie Strauß, Kirchheim-Nabern, 1992, project.
Design for the »The Great Utopia« exhibition, Solomon R. Guggenheim Museum, New York, 1992/93.
Concert hall in Copenhagen, 1993, project.
Lycée Français, London, 1994, project.
Opera house in Cardiff, England, 1994, project.

Arthotel Billie Strauß

Architekten/Architects
Altbau/Existing building: Manfred Strauß, Kirchheim-Nabern
Innenraumgestaltung im Altbau/Interior design in the existing building: Zaha Hadid, London (Mitarbeiter/Collaborator: Patrick Schumacher)
Turm/Tower: Zaha Hadid, London (Mitarbeiter/Collaborator: Patrick Schumacher)

Photograph/Photographer
Bernhard Widmann, Stuttgart

Arthotel Billie Strauß
Weilheimer Straße 18–20
D-73230 Kirchheim-Nabern

T +49-7021-95059-0
F +49-7021-53242